BECAUSE *Manners* MATTER

An A to Z Guide to Etiquette and Social Graces

OLU ADEAGA

The right of Olu Adeaga to be identified as the author of the work has been asserted by her in accordance with the Copyright, Designs and Patents Act, 1988.

All rights reserved.
No part of this publication may be reproduced, stored in a retrieval system, or transmitted in any form or by any means, electronic, mechanical, photocopying, recording or otherwise without prior written permission of the publisher, or in the case of reprographic reproduction in accordance with the terms of licences issued by the Copyright Licensing Agency.

Enquiries concerning reproduction outside these terms should be sent to 'info@jsapphirah.co.uk'

BECAUSE MANNERS MATTER
An A to Z Guide to Etiquette and Social Graces
(Revised Edition)

ISBN: 978-1-912896-05-9

Copyright © March 2020
OLU ADEAGA

Co-Published in the United Kingdom by
JSapphirah, London
&
Syncterface Media, London
~ www.syncterfacemedia.com ~

Design, layout and typesetting by
'Lanre Iroche

Photo Credits:
Adeolu Eletu; Alex Kotliarskyi; Alex Ware; Alvan Nee; Alvaro cvg; Ben White; Bruce Mars; Burgess Milner; Chris Brignola; Christian Stahl; Debby Hudson; Dmitry Tulupov; Fahad Waseem; Glenn Carstens Peters; Guilherme Stecanella; Jon Tyson; Kira Auf Der Heide; Lesly Juarez; Mae Mu; Markus Spiske; Matheus Ferrero; Ryan Crotty; Saltanat Zhursinbek; Sam Dan Truong; Sydney Rae; Artificial photography; bewakoof.com official; christinawocintechchat.com; Heng films; k8; photostockeditor; webaroo.com.au (all on Unsplash)
Additional images from Pexels and Freepik

British Library Cataloguing in Publication Data
A catalogue record for this book is available from the British Library

I am who I am because He says I am.
Thank You for Your Grace

Acknowledgements

This book is dedicated to my father, Abraham Babatunde Fowowe, who taught me about the importance of consideration for others. Although it's been many years since he departed this side of eternity, I am forever grateful to him for sowing the seeds that got me started on this journey of etiquette. I miss you dearly dad; and, PS: I'm now using your crystal glasses for my etiquette training.

I want to appreciate my husband Shola, for his never-ending support for my many projects. Love you very much, my darling.

Also, a huge 'thank you' to my children, Temi and Tubo, who always allow me to practice on them.

To my Spiritual Leaders, Pastors Agu and Sola Irukwu, thank you for your leadership. PAI thank you for pouring into my life these many years, for your constant encouragement, as well as facilitating and nurturing my spiritual growth.

To the people who have collectively helped in shaping this book, I say thank you. Thank you Chizor Akisanya for being there at the beginning. To the co-editors, Sylvia Okuku, Tinuke Akinbulumo and Abiola Awosika; I am truly grateful.

A big 'thank you' to my son, 'Lanre Iroche, who designed and typeset the entire book. To my publisher, Henry Etiaba, I'm grateful for your support and encouragement over the years.

Lastly, to the Esthers' Mentoring Scheme Mentors and Mentees, who supported and encouraged me over the years by sitting through *'The Fabulous Girls' Guide to Etiquette'* sessions at every Shine Woman Retreat; you are truly a fabulous bunch of ladies.

And to everyone who buys or reads this book; do not let anyone convince you otherwise: **Manners Make A Difference**.

Enjoy!

Foreword

"We were created by God to be social beings, and we thrive when our various relationships are rich and fulfilling. If you are someone who wants to behave properly in your interactions with others you come across on a day to day basis, this book is for you. It is a wonderful tool to help us relate with each other in a way that allows us to glorify God as we respect each other. The style is simple, with interesting stories and information which commends it to the reader. A great resource to have in your collection. A must-read."
- Agu Irukwu, Senior Pastor, Jesus House for all nations, Head of The Redeemed Christian Church of God United Kingdom and Northern Ireland, and President (Pentecostal) of Churches Together in England

"Etiquette, or the cultural expectations around the way we behave around others, is essential to building human relationships. Those human relationships - our Relationology - have a bigger effect on our life happiness and business performance than any other factor, so they are worth investing in. If you feel your etiquette needs a polish then read this book."
- Matt Bird, CEO of Relationology International

"In my capacity as a prophet, I have had the privilege of interacting with people in different nations, and I have observed an obvious lack of knowledge of the proper dining etiquette among elite and non-elite alike. But, how do we know the proper way of doing things if we have never been taught? Esther would not have been chosen as queen in the scriptures if she wasn't taught the proper etiquette before she met the king. In this book, Olu Adeaga - 'Princess' - will take you through the protocols, for while we are told that "your gift will make room for you", proper etiquette can justify your presence at the table of opportunity."
- Prophetess Francina Norman

"In a world where manners are a lost art and offense runs rampant because many fail to adhere to the protocols of consideration, this is a timely offering. A fun and easy read, short, sweet and to the point, Olu Adeaga has given the clear cut rules of engagement for every type of situation, from airplane flights to dining, bereavement and everyday lifestyle decisions, in good taste and finesse. So needed, so on point! A must-read for anyone who wants to leave a great and lasting first impression. The perfect gift book and conversation piece to share with others!"
- **Michelle McKinney Hammond**, author of '*The Diva Principle*'

"Etiquette has become an old-fashioned word in these times. It's a word closely associated with rules, and there's nothing my millennial generation hate more than rules. But what Olu Adeaga shows in this concise and profound book is that etiquette is less about rules and more about respect and consideration for others. My favourite entries were G for gratitude, J for jokes and K for kindness."
- **Chibundu Onuzo**, author of '*The Spider King's Daughter*' and '*Welcome to Lagos*'

Contents

Acknowledgments		v
Foreword		vi
Introduction		1
A		7
	Airplane Etiquette	7
	Appreciation	12
	Assertiveness	13
	Attitude	14
B		15
	Bereavement	15
	Blog Etiquette	17
	Borrowing	18
	Business Etiquette	19
C		21
	Cards	21
	Common Courtesy	22
	Complaints	23
	Compliment	24
	Conversation	26
D		29
	Dieting	29
	Dining Etiquette	30
	Dogs	34
	Dress Etiquette	36
E		40
	Effortless Style	40
	Elegance	41
	Email Etiquette	42
	Entertaining Guests	43
F		45
	Fashion	45
	Flatmates	46
	Fragrance	47
	Friends	48
	Funerals	49
G		50
	Gifts	50
	Grace	52
	Gratitude	54
	Grooming Regime	55

H 57
- Hair 57
- Handshakes 58
- Hospitality 59
- Houseguests 60
- Humour 61

I 62
- Integrity 62
- Interviews 62
- Introductions 65
- Invitations 66

J 68
- Jabber 68
- Jealousy 69
- Jeans 70
- Jokes 71

K 73
- Kindness 73
- Kissing 74
- Know-it-alls 75

L 77
- Language 77
- Letter Writing 78
- Love 80

M 81
- Make-up 81
- Manners 82
- Mind Your Language 83

N 84
- Neighbours 84
- No 85
- Notes 86

O 87
- Office Etiquette 87
- Order/Organised 88
- Original 89

P 91
- Patience 91
- Perfume 91
- Please 92
- Punctuality 92

Q 94
- Quality 94
- Quarrels 94
- Queuing 95

R   97
- Respect/Regard   97
- Restaurants   98
- Restroom   99
- Riches   101

S   102
- Sales   102
- Sincerity   103
- Spaghetti   105

T   107
- Table Setting   107
- Texting   107
- Thank you   108
- Tipping   109
- Tolerance   110
- Travel   111
- Trust   112

U   114
- Unappreciated   114
- Unapproachable   114
- Underwear   115

V   117
- Versatility   117
- Visiting   117
- Volume   118

W   120
- Wardrobe Maintenance   120
- Wedding Etiquette   121

X   123
- Xenophobia   123
- Xmas   123

Y   125
- Yawning   125
- Yes   126

Z   127
- Zeal   127
- Zebra Crossings   127
- Zips   128

Conclusion   131
About the Author   133

Introduction

On a flight to New York one day, what started as a relatively routine trip ended up being a thought-provoking exercise, which inspired the idea for this book.

About an hour into the flight, the flight attendants started serving the main in-flight meal; I could not wait to start, as I was famished. Then out of the corner of my eye, I caught a glimpse of the lady to my right grab her bread roll, take the first bite into it and then started gnawing at it. I was traumatised, to say the least. Why was I so perturbed by her actions, you ask? It must have been because I was not expecting such. In my little corner of the world, I feel that there must be a standard way of doing things – particularly in public places and in our interactions with others - which she knowingly or unknowingly was not adhering to.

Contrast this with another experience at a crowded upscale restaurant where we were seated close to another table. I could not help but notice a family of five – father, mother and three children. The child that caught my attention was about 9 years old. Each time the waitress came to ask what the family required, the child's responses were always punctuated with "yes please," "no, thank you," "yes, thank you," etc. This display of courtesy towards someone serving their needs came as a pleasant and, yet again, thought-provoking surprise.

So, in a society where constant interactions are the order of the day, what is the right way to behave or do things, or better still, what is the right etiquette? And if there is such a thing as the right etiquette, who knows what it is? I have always been very passionate about etiquette (the right way to do things in social interactions), and these two recent experiences served as catalysts in deciding to journey down the rabbit hole and write down my thoughts on the A to Z guide to etiquette and social graces.

Origin of Etiquette

Etiquette dates back to the 18th century, from the court of Louis XIV, the King of France. The King had a gardener, who observed that the nobles and aristocrats who visited the King often walked on the grass in the palace grounds. To prevent this repetitive occurrence, he put up signs or étiquets that read, "Keep off the grass", to deter them from walking on the grass in the grounds. However, the aristocrats ignored the notices and continued to walk on the grass. To put a stop to this blatant disregard, the King issued a decree, which stated that no one was to walk beyond the boundaries of the étiquets (the signs or notices). The word étiquet later evolved to describe the tickets or small cards that were given to people who were invited to court functions. These cards contained instructions on how to behave properly in court during such functions.

Definition of Etiquette

The Oxford dictionary defines etiquette as "the customary code of polite behaviour in society or among members of a particular profession or group." In its simplest form, etiquette refers to those rules that shape how we behave in society. It is the conventional norm, an unwritten code that evolves from written rules.

In a world where we interact with each other in many different ways, etiquette is all about being polite and well mannered.

Two words undergird the principle of etiquette. They are **'respect' and 'consideration'** for others. As mentioned earlier, the word etiquette refers to rules that shape interactive behaviour. When we hear the word 'rules', it may get our backs up, as rules often tend to do. However, if we bear in mind the two words 'respect' and 'consideration', etiquette suddenly becomes easier to embrace and adopt. The reason is that every single human being wants to be valued and treated with respect.

There is a saying; "We are free to do all things, but there are things which are not wise to do. We are free to do all things, but not all things are for the common good." (The Bible: 1 Corinthians 10:23 – *Basic English Translation*)

While etiquette refers to the rules (appropriate manners) that shape our interactions, we must also understand the more modern concept of social skills and graces.

What are Social Skills and Graces?

The Collins dictionary defines social skills as "the skills that are necessary in order to communicate and interact with others."

Social skills are the skills we need or should have to get along with other people. The skills we use to interact in social situations are known as social graces. They include manners, deportment and fashion. Nowadays, there is an increased emphasis on acquiring social skills, particularly in the corporate world, because appropriate social skills enable us to communicate, persuade, interact, relate and socialize with other members of society effectively without undue disharmony or divergence.

Social skills are often demonstrated in both verbal and non-verbal ways. Sadly, the reality of life is that people will often judge you by the presence or absence of such skills. The skills we have or lack are often what others use to determine our status, assess us as potential friends or partners, and consider us for employment or promotion in the workplace.

In this A to Z guide to etiquette and social graces, I have chosen a few 'rules, signs, notices, norms' and social graces that I feel are important in our daily interactions with others in the 21st century. The guide is organised in alphabetical order, to make it easier to find advice on specific topics relating to etiquette and social graces, ranging from the subject of Airplane etiquette all the way through to the matter of Zips. The idea behind this book is to guide you and help you understand the proper way to behave and do things in modern society. Even though it is the 21st century, where people seem to be pleasing themselves and doing away with certain customs, I believe it still pays to have good manners. Being courteous, considerate and respectful will take you far and will bring you a step closer to success in life.

If you know the appropriate way to behave in all situations, you will be better able to adapt to various circumstances and may save yourself from much embarrassment and awkwardness. As a result, you will find that people will have more respect and regard for you. Knowing the expected way to behave in different situations will not only save you from what could be embarrassing and awkward situations but will also make you feel much better about yourself. The ability to adapt to various situations is a skill that attracts respect.

Etiquette is not about being pretentious; which is defined and characterized by: "an assumption of dignity or importance, especially when exaggerated or undeserved; or making an exaggerated outward show; being ostentatious." - *dictionary.com*. Neither is it about pretending to be who you are not.

On the contrary, etiquette and social graces are about becoming a better and more pleasant 'you', particularly as we interact with other people. Etiquette and social graces are about positively impacting other people's lives and making them feel good about themselves.

You will probably agree with me that the modern world we now live has become increasingly selfish and self-centred. Conversely, etiquette is about thinking about others and how our actions impact their lives.

At the end of the day, there is nothing near as fulfilling as leaving a smile on someone's face as a result of their interaction with you. So, welcome to this journey through the world of etiquette and social graces.

"In a world where we interact with each other in many different ways, etiquette is all about being polite and well mannered"

An **A to Z Guide** to Etiquette and Social Graces

A

Airplane Etiquette

AIRPLANES HAVE BECOME A common and very convenient means of travel, whether for business or pleasure. When travelling by plane, we will have to share a small enclosed space for several hours with others. As a result, there are several etiquette/rules to consider and imbibe that describes the right way to behave:

- Do not jump the queue/line. Most airlines try to board passengers in order. Listen for the announcement. If you miss the announcement, ask the counter staff. Regardless of the class, you are travelling, you do not want to rush to the front of the queue/line only to be told that they are just boarding mothers and babies.

- There is a reason why airlines state that only one cabin bag is allowed per passenger; it can be very frustrating to arrive at your seat only to find the overhead compartment above your seat full of someone else's multiple belongings. When placing your belongings in the overhead compartment, consider the person that will come after you. Remember - etiquette is about respect and consideration for others.
- Travelling with children is often hard work and the stress of it should not be underestimated. Children will be children, and for most, being cooped up in a small space for several hours can be quite challenging. For people travelling without children, being seated near a child or within hearing distance of a screaming child may very quickly end up spoiling their journey. Therefore, try to find ways of entertaining the children so that they do not disturb other passengers.
- Having ample sources of distraction in the form of toys, games, books, puzzles, snacks, etc., on hand should go a long way. Children (especially toddlers) are pretty volatile and easily excitable and may wish to run around the plane, which can be exacerbated by boredom experienced on long flights. Ensure you take time to carefully elucidate that the plane is not a playground and the need to be considerate of other passengers.
- If you are sitting beside someone, let your child know that the person should not be disturbed and, most importantly, that their possessions be left untouched, unless offered to them. Except they love babies, a baby that cries persistently next to a passenger is easily any passenger's greatest nightmare. Therefore, consciously find ways to soothe your baby as effectively as possible. For most babies, cabin pressure is an obvious culprit as it is known to hurt the ears, so feeding them might help. The sucking motion helps to relieve the pressure in their ears.

- Ignoring the child is an absolute NO-NO. No matter how tempting ignoring the child may seem at the time, it is not advisable, as this may accelerate the irritation of the other passengers, who may start thinking that you do not care about others. Last word on travelling with children: if you are the parent, it is your responsibility to maintain order out of consideration for others.
- In most aeroplanes, you are now able to recline your seat for better comfort. Please be aware of your fellow passenger behind you. When the in-flight meal is being served, your seat should be in the upright position to allow the person behind you to eat properly. If the person in front of you has their seat reclined, you can politely ask them to put it up. In the event of a refusal, politely inform the air steward. Remember to look behind you before reclining your seat.
- A plane is a small confined space, and etiquette requires we respect our fellow passenger's personal space. Watch your elbow and do not hog the armrest. It would be a good idea to bring your reading material on board, not everyone enjoys the idea of sharing their magazines with strangers.
- If you have to take off your shoes, please check before removing them, that your feet are not smelly. It is advisable to always have a fresh pair of socks for the plane in the odd event that your feet do smell. Alternatively, you could simply keep your shoes on.
- It is advisable to have some deodorant, perfume or aftershave handy, in the event, you start to notice you smell sweaty. You are probably not going to be told (out of politeness) that you are the source of discomfort and distress to others because you smell bad. However, it behoves you to think about others when you sweat and more likely than not, emit an odour. In some cases, some people are not aware that they emit body odour

(or may have a precipitating medical condition). It is, however, good practise to always ensure that you have used a deodorant appropriately before you board a plane.
- While this may be more difficult for some than others, try not to sleep on your neighbour's shoulder. If you know that you snore especially loudly, perhaps you could apologise in anticipation of the impending disruption to be caused (on a light note) to your neighbour at the start of the flight. To spare your embarrassment, there are now several different products available on the market for snorers, which might be worth investing in. These include nasal strips, which help to open the nasal passages; throat spray, which is meant to lubricate the soft tissue at the back of the throat to reduce the vibrations that cause snoring; and if your snoring is causing you distress there is also the option to have surgery. Alternatively, you could simply forgo sleep and watch a movie or read a book for the duration of the flight.
- If listening to music, make sure you wear headphones and keep the volume down because your neighbour might still be able to hear the music.
- Do not force people into a conversation with you, particularly if they look like they do not want to chat. If you do end up talking to other people, please keep your voice(s) down. Remember, someone else may be trying to sleep.
- Be conscious of how much alcohol you are consuming - if you are going to drink alcohol at all. Airlines now have stricter guidelines on the excessive consumption of alcohol. If you are found to be drunk or behaving inappropriately, you will not be allowed to fly. Pilots have been known to take a detour or even fly back to the original airport to remove drunk and disorderly passengers from the aircraft. This can cause serious delays and much inconvenience. Have consideration for your fellow

passengers when you are drinking alcohol. If you know that alcohol makes you aggressive, rowdy or sick, limit your alcohol consumption.

- If you do feel sick during the flight, try to make sure you can get to the restroom. If this is not possible, make sure you use the in-flight sick bags provided – your neighbours will not be impressed if you were to regurgitate your dinner all over them.
- Ensure that you leave the lavatory as clean as you found it. Wipe the toilet seat after use before flushing the loo and remember to close the toilet lid before flushing. Also, wipe the sink after washing your hands. Endeavour to dispose of any tissue residue lying around.
- Take care when retrieving luggage from the overhead compartments.
- Be careful if you are carrying a backpack when boarding or leaving the plane. People have been known to blunder down the aisles swinging heavy backpacks around on their backs, unaware that their fellow passengers are being battered by the hefty luggage. Be conscious of who is around you; there may be little children who could end up being seriously hurt if struck hard by a heavy backpack. It is probably better to carry your luggage in front of you to avoid bumping into other passengers.
- Be considerate when leaving the plane; do not push other passengers in an attempt to leave the plane before them.
- Prepare to assist other passengers who may need help, i.e. the elderly and those with children.

"Travel teaches toleration" - *Benjamin Disraeli*

Appreciation

DICTIONARY.COM DEFINES THE word 'appreciate' as "to be grateful and thankful for something or to someone. It could also be a way of showing how much you value someone or something."

Other definitions include:
- To recognize the quality, significance, or magnitude of i.e. "appreciated their freedom."
- To be thankful or show gratitude for: i.e. "I appreciate your help."
- To admire greatly; value: i.e. *"pay a compliment when appropriate."*

We all have to relate to people, and our relationships are what enrich our lives. It is therefore important to value our relationships in addition to letting people around us know how much we value them. Generally, we live in a world where people feel 'entitled', the result of which makes them feel that they do not have to show any appreciation when they receive things. However, as a courteous and well-mannered person, you should still show that you are grateful or thankful irrespective of the size, price or even if the thing, action or gift is expected. Even if you feel that the person knows you appreciate them, a practical show of appreciation is always a thoughtful gesture.

You can show your appreciation in many ways: with a phone call, a written letter, an email, a text, or in-person with a hug or a smile, or you can find ways to return a favour. The most important thing is to let the person know that you are grateful or thankful for whatever it is that they may have done.

This etiquette is particularly important when we are being served by apparent strangers in the day; be it the bus driver, the postman, the train ticket collector, the corner shop attendant, or the restaurant waitress; the list goes on.

Please be aware that any display of appreciation should be honest and sincere.

> **"Appreciation is a wonderful thing: It makes what is excellent in others belong to us as well"** - *Voltaire*

Assertiveness

SOMETIMES PEOPLE MISTAKE AGGRESSION for assertiveness. Being assertive should never make the other person feel threatened, while being aggressive may well do that.

To be assertive is to be self-assured and confident. It means that you can firmly and confidently state your opinion or ensure that your rights are acknowledged. However, you can be assertive without trampling on the rights of others. You can respectfully assert your opinion or rights which shows that you understand that others have rights and opinions also and that you are not living alone on a desert island.

And Yes! It is possible to be assertive and still follow the rules of etiquette. Being assertive means you can express your views clearly and articulately without being aggressive. The thing to remember is not to be rude whilst being assertive. I would say be assertive with a smile on your face; this can be a very powerful weapon for getting a message across.

"The basic difference between being assertive and being aggressive is how our words and behaviour affect the rights and well-being of others." - *Sharon Anthony Bower*

Attitude

THE COLLINS DICTIONARY SAYS "Your attitude to something is the way that you think and feel about it, especially when this shows in the way you behave. Other definitions of attitude are manner, disposition, feeling, position, etc., with regard to a person or thing; tendency or orientation, especially of the mind: a negative attitude; group attitudes.

Concerning attitude and etiquette, always remember that you have a choice. You can choose to have a negative or positive attitude towards things or people. The number one rule is that you have the power of choice, which simply means that you do not allow other people or circumstances to determine how you behave or feel. However, as a rule, of etiquette, you will go a long way in life if you have a positive and good attitude towards people and things, and it will stand you in good stead.

"Attitude is a little thing that makes a big difference".
- Winston Churchill

B

Bereavement

WHEN SOMEONE LOSES A thing or person they love, be it a friend, family member, colleague or even a family pet, it can be a very traumatic and difficult time for them. In such situations, it can be difficult to know what to say or do. The number one thing to bear in mind is that people handle loss differently.

If the bereaved is very close to you, it may help to visit them if you are available. In the event you are short of words, a simple gesture like a hug goes a long way in comforting the bereaved.

Remember that it is not what you say but what you do that matters.

- Do not grieve louder than the bereaved out of respect and consideration. When you visit the home of the bereaved,

respect the atmosphere and conduct in the home.
- Do not talk endlessly about the deceased but follow the lead of the bereaved. Be kind to the bereaved and respond sensitively to their sorrow.
- If you have to write a note or send a card, avoid telling the bereaved that it was "God's will" or that "they will get over it."

In many cases, it may be helpful if you can anticipate the needs of the bereaved, e.g. help to make meals, do the grocery shopping, tend to their children, take the children to school if they are not up to it, etc. Also, helping to prepare for the funeral and all other necessary arrangements may be a welcome relief to the bereaved. Conversely, although it is a caring gesture to help people in their time of need, try to be sensitive to what they are going through and avoid being too pushy.

Be aware that the bereaved might want to be left alone to deal with their grief, or they may not want you to take over the arrangements. Try to gauge when it is best to help and when it is better to back away. If they are emotionally capable of making decisions, ask them first if there is anything they would like you to help with.

It is not unusual that in the immediate days following the death of a loved one, the bereaved may not remember much.

Be tolerant of any behaviour by the bereaved that may be out of character. As mentioned earlier, people handle loss differently.

If you are not close to the bereaved or are out of town, it is appropriate to send a card, hand-written note, text or an email. The bereaved party or parties will welcome a message of condolence in any form.

"The friend who can be silent with us in a moment of despair or confusion, who can stay with us in an hour of grief and bereavement, who can tolerate not knowing... not healing, not curing... that is a friend who cares." - *Henri Nouwen*

Blog Etiquette

A BLOG IS DEFINED AS a website containing a writer's or group of writers' own experiences, observations, opinions, etc., often having images and links to other webpages.

Rules to observe:

- If you do not want the world to see it, do not post it.
- Always state that it is your opinion, even if you are an authority on the subject.
- Do not take any comment posted on your blog as personal; you may disagree with the comment, but this does not mean that you have to be rude or disrespectful.
- Never post someone else's words as yours without asking for permission to do so. If you have to use another person's

work, acknowledge them and give credit to them. It helps to be original.
- If a person takes time to post comments on your blog, courtesy demands that you respond/acknowledge their post, even if it is just to say thank you.
- Stick to the post and do not get sidetracked by other comments posted on your blog. Remember focus! Focus!!

"Don't focus on having a great blog. Focus on producing a blog that's great for your readers." - Brian Clark

Borrowing

THERE ARE THREE RULES regarding borrowing;
a. You should always ask for permission to borrow something and never just assume that it is ok.
b. Do not borrow unless you are sure that you will return the item.
c. Make sure you return the item in the same (exact) condition as when it was lent to you.

Borrowing has been known to cause friction between friends

Asking to borrow certain things is a No-No. Do not ask to borrow your friend's car if you know you are not insured to drive the vehicle. Remember that etiquette is about consideration and respect for the other person, so avoid actions that have the potential to put others at a disadvantage – even friends.

Do not borrow money if you can help it. If you have to borrow money, make sure it is a reasonable amount and you have a clear and definite means to repay it. If you have agreed a time in which to repay the amount and there is likely to be a delay, be courteous enough to let your friend know as soon as possible. Do not wait until you are asked.

- If you have to borrow items, it is not a good idea to borrow a brand-new item that has not been used by the owner.
- If you borrow an item, do not lend it to someone else.
- If you borrow an item and it is lost or damaged, offer to pay for it or replace it.
- If you regularly borrow an item, you should offer to pay for the upkeep.

Ladies, do not borrow items of clothing from just about anyone. Sisters and 'bestest' friends are the exceptions.

> **"Before borrowing money from a friend, decide which you need more."** - *Addison H. Hallock*

Business Etiquette

BUSINESS ETIQUETTE IS CONCERNED with how to behave and conduct oneself in the business world or any business situation or environment. This cuts across the board, whether you are a business owner (the boss) or an employee.

In a business environment, always be considerate and courteous to the people you work for, work with, or who work for you. Be polite and pleasant to everyone you come into contact with, even people who may be in a junior position to you in the workplace. It may amaze you to find out that these people have more power than is credited to them, for they can be a hindrance or a help to your business success or career. Rudeness should never be demonstrated or tolerated.

One important rule regarding business etiquette is to build relationships with people. It helps if you are considerate towards others and do your utmost to avoid any misunderstandings. If you are unsure about anything, it is wise to clarify the matter before proceeding.

To succeed in the business world, you need the following:

- Good manners.
- Integrity: If you commit to something, see it through.
- Confidentiality: Be trustworthy and reliable in private matters.
- Sensitivity to people's feelings: Never put anyone down. Never be rude. Always try to be polite and courteous.
- Appropriate dressing: Find out about the dress code for the workplace and any business event and dress in an appropriate manner.
- Ability to network: Build relationships with the people you work with, find out about their families, hobbies, etc.
- Knowledge of business etiquette and customs: When carrying out business internationally, always find out about the business etiquette and customs in that country. Read up about the country, the people and how they conduct business. It would be a bonus if you learn how to greet in their language.

It helps if you carry your business card with you. If asked for your telephone number, it looks very unprofessional to have to look for a paper to write it on.

"In the end, all business operations can be reduced to three words: people, product and profits. Unless you've got a good team, you can't do much with the other two." - *Lee Iacocca*

C

Cards

WHEN BUYING A CARD for someone, e.g. a birthday, wedding or get well card, etc., make sure you read the words in the card first. Before you make a purchase, determine that the words will be appropriate for the person you want to give the card to. It is not only about what you like, but also about whether the person will appreciate it. For example, if you are a Christian and you want to give a birthday card to someone who is not of the same faith as you, choose carefully because you do not want to offend the receiver.

    I find that I appreciate cards that have handwritten notes. To me, it sends the message that the person thought about me whilst writing the note.

Lastly, you do not have to spend a fortune on a card. Most cards are thrown away after a few days anyway, so why not get a plain card and write your own words inside. The cards that I have kept over the years are those that have been handwritten.

> **"And I always keep cards people send me. I have a whole wall covered with them."** - *Emma Watson*

> **"I squirrel away sealed greeting cards that people give me, so I can open them later when I'm having a bad day."** - *Emily Procter*

Common Courtesy

COMMON MEANS SOMETHING THAT happens or occurs frequently. Courtesy is defined as "excellence of manners or social conduct, i.e. polite behaviour." It is also defined as "a courteous, respectful, or considerate act or expression." - *dictionary.com*

Keenan De Barros of Harmer PR noted on her blog that: "common courtesy is a bit like common sense – it is not common. Along with politeness and manners, it seems to have died with the dinosaurs. I'm not talking about standing up when a lady enters the room or helping elderly people cross the road. Let's start with the simple 'please', 'excuse me' and 'thank you' – before they altogether disappear from our collective vocabulary."

She goes on to elucidate that: "respect permeates everything – our work lives, our personal lives, our social lives and all things that surround us. But as we scratch our heads over the problem of hoodlum teenagers and their antisocial habits and ponder how to inject a bit of respect into the adolescent population, maybe we should start looking a bit closer to home.

It is easy to forget the small acts of kindness we witness every day

— when people stop to let you out of a side road, when the bus driver waits whilst you run to the bus and when the shopkeeper smiles as he hands you the morning paper. But if we paid more attention to these good turns and made it our personal daily resolution to do something nice or simply be courteous, maybe we can encourage mutual respect. Surely there is some truth in the mantra that 'what goes around comes around." - *Keenan De Barros*

I couldn't agree more!

> **"Among the qualities of mind and heart which conduce to worldly success, there is one, the importance of which is more real, and which is generally underrated in our day...It is courtesy."**
> *- Herbert Schiffer*

Complaints

A COMPLAINT IS AN expression of discontent, regret, pain, censure, resentment, or grief. It is also a cause of discontent, lamentation, etc. - *dictionary.com*

Occasionally, we may be discontent with a level of service or when sold a defective product. We might complain about a rude member of staff, an undercooked meal, a misplaced order etc. Most times, when we complain, it is usually because our expectations have not been met or satisfied.

Ideally, we should complain to right a wrong, which may benefit others, and also to allow the company or business the opportunity to correct the problem.

If you have to complain, try to stay calm and avoid yelling, shouting, cussing, or screaming. If you do, you are unlikely to get any result, and the people involved will most likely be put off by your behaviour.

There are keys to complaining:

- Know who to complain to — It is usually best to speak to someone in authority. However, you should always try to resolve the issue with the person you have a problem with.
- Know where and when to complain - For example, when dining with others at a restaurant, making bad remarks about the food or the service in front of others will not solve anything but will only make you look bad. If you have a complaint, excuse yourself and talk to the manager or host discreetly; they are the ones equipped to handle such issues. Initiate your complaint with extreme politeness and a smile; this is probably the best way to win the other person over to your side. If you are dissatisfied with the food, say so discreetly and with minimal fuss, and request any necessary (and reasonable) changes be made. Keep things pleasant, and do not shoot the messenger. Be aware that excessive complaining may spoil your companions' evening.
- If you have to write a letter of complaint, make sure it is short, concise and clear. Ensure it is addressed to the person at the top if you know their name. Avoid rambling. Limit it to a page at the maximum.
- Do not complain all the time; you will become known as a whiner.

"If you have time to whine and complain about something, then you have the time to do something about it." - *Anthony J. D'Angelo*

Compliment

DICTIONARY.COM DEFINES A COMPLIMENT as "an expression of praise, commendation, or admiration; a sincere compliment that boosts one's morale; a formal act or expression of civility, respect, or regard; a courteous greeting; good wishes; regards."

Pay people compliments

A great way to build social skills is with compliments. Every human being wants to feel appreciated; we all love praise. Complimenting people can be a tricky matter because, first and foremost, you want to come across as being sincere. The last thing you want is to be perceived as a flatterer. Therefore, be conscious of 'over complimenting'.

When paying compliments, make statements that you know to be true and stay with the specifics. Try complimenting someone on their achievements, e.g. if they have just completed a task successfully. When paying compliments, make sure that you look the person in the eyes and smile; this will make you come across as sincere.

There are polite and decent ways to say things. For example, saying "You look good in that dress" is more complimentary than "I like how that dress looks on you". An even more complimentary way would be to say, "You make that dress look good."

A genuine compliment will make the recipient feel good about themself, and this will earn you more points in the social scene. But please, only offer genuine compliments.

Lastly, avoid double-edged compliments. A double-edged compliment is when you give a compliment with one hand and take it away with the other. For example, "Wow, well done, I heard you got that job; did your dad put in a word for you?"

Recipients should acknowledge a compliment with a "thank you" and a smile. If someone says you look good in an outfit, a simple "thank you" will suffice; there is no need to give the history of where you bought the dress, how much you paid for the shirt, or that the shoes were a bargain.

A well-paid compliment will almost certainly leave the recipient happier and with a warm feeling.

"Too often we underestimate the power of a touch, a smile, a kind word, a listening ear, an honest compliment, or the smallest act of caring, all of which have the potential to turn a life around."
- *Leo F. Buscaglia*

Conversation

A CONVERSATION IS "the ability to talk socially with others: informal interchange of thoughts, information, etc. by spoken words; oral communication between persons; talk; colloquy." – *dictionary.com*

The art of making conversation
The following are the necessary skills required when making

conversation with other people:
- Ask appropriate questions: When you are socialising, it is important to realise that you are not in a debate, and you should steer away from questions that might cause tension or controversy.
- You do not want to cause a scene, so ask appropriate questions for the situation at hand; comment on the décor and other surface topics that will keep the conversation going but will not cause any tension or anger to flare up.
- Always be aware of your surroundings and be conscious of who you are talking to.
- Keep it Short: In social situations, it is always important to understand the nature of social etiquette in conversation. Keep conversations short, and socialise with everyone present. If you have a long, in-depth conversation with certain individuals, they might be resentful, because they may be interested in exchanging pleasantries with the other people in attendance.
- Take turns when talking: For example, you talk for a bit, then I talk for a bit; I ask a question and wait for a reply; I show some interest in your reply.
- Make 'small talk': be able to chat about unimportant topics.
- Listen: It is essential to take notice of what others are saying and avoid talking over people.
- Respond: Nod and smile to indicate that you are following the conversation.

Remember that at most social events, there is the likelihood that you will be meeting people for the first time. You have to be mindful of what you say and take care not to ask questions that might offend. For example, it would not be wise to blurt out something like, "Are you pregnant?" For all you know, the person you are speaking to may just have a flabby tummy or a medical condition such as large fibroids or may have been trying to get pregnant for a long time and your question reminds them of the pain. It is also a good idea to gather more information about people before you disclose personal information about yourself or ask personal questions.

Remember, social etiquette is keeping conversation pleasant and short.

"Conversation should be pleasant without scurrility, witty without affectation, free without indecency, learned without conceitedness, novel without falsehood." - *William Shakespeare*

"One of the best rules in conversation is, never to say a thing which any of the company can reasonably wish had been left unsaid."
- Jonathan Swift

D

Dieting

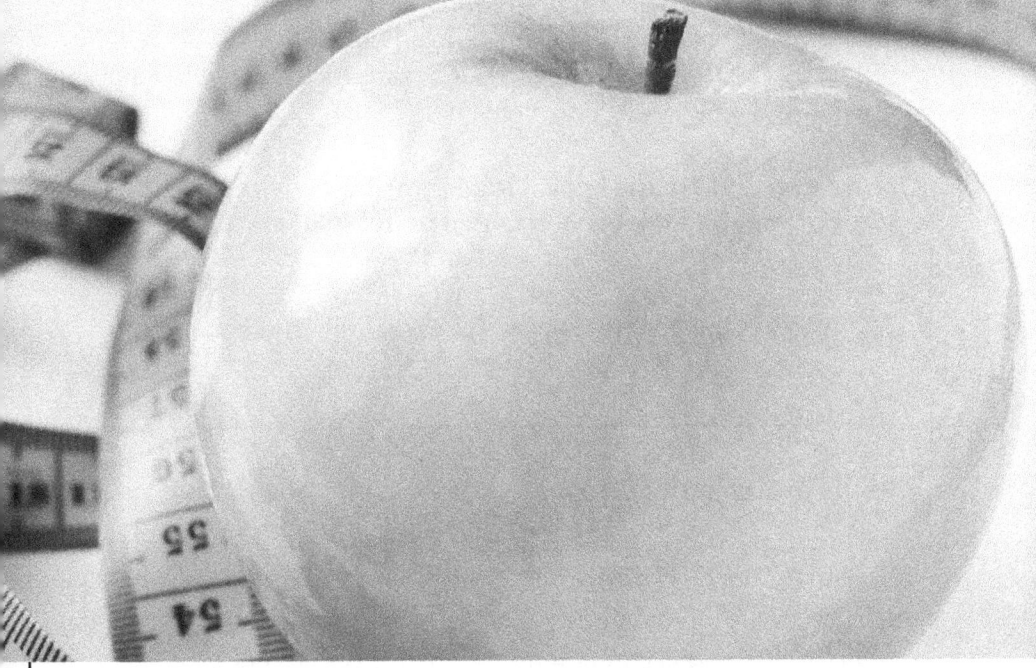

STATISTICS OBTAINED BY ANALYST Mintel showed that 1 in 4 adults are constantly trying to lose weight. Of these, 2 in 5, which represents 37% of women, were dieting most of the time.

So, what is diet etiquette? It is a rule that governs how you behave or conduct yourself when dieting. A few points to note about dieting etiquette:

- If you are the one dieting, please do not inflict your diet on others. Just because you may only be able to eat certain foods, should not mean that others must do the same. Remember, consideration for others!
- If invited to a party, do not expect your host to cater especially

for you because you are on a diet.
- Avoid moaning or talking endlessly about your diet. You chose to go on the diet, so do not expect sympathy from others.
- Try not to be a boring know-it-all diet expert who rambles on about the latest diet crazes.
- Lastly, if you have friends who are dieting, encourage them as best as you can. Be considerate and not tempt them with your actions or words

"I tried every diet in the book. I tried some that weren't in the book. I tried eating the book. It tasted better than most diets."
- Dolly Parton

"A diet is the penalty we pay for exceeding the feed limit."
- Unknown

Dining Etiquette

UNLESS YOU WERE BORN into royalty or went to finishing school, most people are intimidated by a formal dinner, because there are many more crockery and silverware on the table than are used in everyday dining. A formal table is usually set out as follows:
- Right side - knives, spoons and glasses
- Left side – forks and napkin
- Above the plate – dessert spoon and fork
- To the left-hand side, slightly above the plate - is the side plate with the bread and knife.

Each course has its own set of cutlery, but the cutlery will be laid out in the order in which it will be used. Therefore, always use the outer cutlery when you are served the next course. You do not necessarily need to know what a fish fork looks like – all you need to know is that when the fish is served, the appropriate fork will be the one that is the

outermost on your left. If you are still unsure what to do with a dish, wait and observe what your host does. Some foods are properly eaten with your fingers (like artichoke hearts), but when in doubt, use the cutlery.

When eating your napkin should be placed on your lap. It is returned to the table only at the end of the meal when everyone is finished, not when you are finished. The napkin is used to dab around the corners of your mouth, not to wipe your mouth.

Once you use your cutlery, never put it back on the table; always rest it on your plate.

How you place your knife and fork will signal to the server whether you have finished eating or whether you are resting between courses. To indicate that you have not finished eating but are only taking a rest, make an "X" over your plate by placing the fork on the left and the knife on the right in the 'X' position.

To indicate that you are done with your meal, place the knife and fork together diagonally with the lower side on the right and the higher side at 11 o'clock.

Note that at a formal dinner, you cannot begin your meal until everyone has been served. You should also observe the following etiquette:

- Keep the correct posture at the table. Your back should be straight, your shoulders should not be hunched and your arms should be at your side. Do not put your elbows on the table whilst eating.
- Pay attention to your drink. Look into your glass while you drink instead of over it.
- Do not talk with food in your mouth. Take small bites of your food; this way it will be easier for you to participate in the conversation and avoid talking with your mouth full. Also, try to eat at a slow, relaxed pace.
- Sip your beverage after you have swallowed your food, this way your mouth will not look fuller than it should. If the food in your mouth is very hot, you can take a small sip of water.
- Discreetly use your fingers to remove any strange objects from your mouth and put them at the edge of the plate. Do not spit them on the napkin or the plate.
- Move your soup spoon from the front of the bowl away from you to gather a spoonful. Carefully bring this to your mouth and tip the soup in from the side of the spoon. Do not suck or slurp. Tilt the bowl away from you to gather the last of the soup on your spoon. Place your spoon down while you break off pieces of bread. Your spoon should be left in the bowl, not on the side plate when you have finished.
- To the left side of a place setting will be a side plate on which bread rolls will be placed. You should break your roll into bite-sized pieces that should be eaten individually. Rather than

either taken from the butter dish and placed on the edge of your side plate. Each piece of bread should be individually buttered rather than buttering many pieces at the same time.

Absolutely Do Nots:
- Do not announce your need to go to the restroom; nobody needs to know that while eating. Excuse yourself and leave discreetly.
- Do not groom or touch your hair at the table. Your head should not be scratched while at the table. Excuse yourself and head to the restroom instead.
- Personal belongings like briefcases, telephones, pagers and purses should not be placed on the table. You may place small items on your lap and larger items near your feet.
- Do not overload your plate with food. Try a little of everything without overloading your plate and only add an amount of food that makes your plate look barely full. If, after you finish, you are still hungry, you may then put more food on your plate.
- Do not reach across the table. Ask the person near the desired item to pass it to you. Food is usually passed to the right. The only exception to this is if you are asked by the person to your immediate left to pass the dish; it makes no sense to pass it to the right in this case.
- Do not put the knife in your mouth, no matter how tasty the dish is. Sometimes, as an involuntary response to the taste of the food, people are tempted to lick their knives. It may seem easier to just lick the knife or to take food from the knife, but make sure you use the right cutlery instead.
- Do not blow on hot food. First, it draws attention to you, and second, it gives the impression that you are in a hurry to eat. Wait until your food cools down enough so that you can eat it. Start with the top layers of food on your plate. The soup should

be stirred until it cools down.
- Whilst eating, do not chew with your mouth open, nor smack your lips. Making noises while eating is very unpleasant and shows a lack of consideration for the other guests at the table.
- Under no circumstance should you make gestures with cutlery. If you need to make a gesture, ensure you rest your spoon, fork or knife first.
- When you are done with your meal, do not push your plate away from you; leave the plate where it is for the waiter/server to collect.
- Accidents are bound to happen. In the event food or drink spills on our clothes, resist the urge to wipe the stain using water from your glass. Politely excuse yourself and attend to the stain in the restroom.
- As previously noted, the napkin is provided to dab at the corners of your mouth and not to wipe your face.

"Good manners: The noise you don't make when you're eating soup." - *Bennett Cerf*

"Manners are a sensitive awareness of the feelings of others. If you have that awareness, you have good manners, no matter which fork you use." - *Emily Post*

Dogs

HAVING AND KEEPING A DOG is a huge responsibility. It is important to bear this in mind when deciding whether to get one. Not everyone cares about dogs (however mortifying that may seem to dog lovers); do not, therefore, assume that everyone will adore your little 'fur-baby'.

It is important to make sure that your dog is well trained, well behaved and can socialise. Remember, etiquette is about respect and consideration for others.

- When walking your dog, it is your responsibility to clean up any mess it makes. It is advisable to carry plastic bags with you at all times so that you can pick up and dispose of any mess. Most countries have a strict policy for the disposal of animal waste in public spaces, violation of which will attract a fine.
- Please keep your dog under control at all times. If necessary, use a lead, especially when there are people, particularly children, around. This is so important because even the tamest dog has been known to go crazy when provoked. It also helps to make sure that your dog is properly trained. The law in most developed countries treats dog attacks very seriously. If a dog is dangerously out of control, the owner may be fined, prosecuted, banned from owning dogs in the future, or the offending dog may be put down.
- Always ask if dogs are allowed in places, e.g. parties, other people's homes, etc.

> "What counts is not necessarily the size of the dog in the fight - it's the size of the fight in the dog." - *Dwight D. Eisenhower*

Dress Etiquette

THE REALITY OF LIFE is that people judge you by the way you are dressed. Being attired in the correct clothing can mean the difference between comfort in a certain situation and feeling out of place.

It is a good idea for a lady to carry a shawl/scarf/shrug. You might need to cover your modesty or the weather might simply change and you need to cover up.

Gentlemen should have a clean handkerchief on hand, not just for personal use but it may be handy if a lady should otherwise need it.

Clothing need not be garish; it is courteous to others to avoid attracting attention to yourself. Think of the word 'modest', which means that your clothes are simple, reasonable and suit the occasion.

Being stylish is about making sure your appearance is smart, elegant and that you are bold enough to create your style.

Bottom line is to avoid following fashion or fad slavishly.

> **"No elegant woman follows fashion slavishly."** - *Christian Dior*

The older we get, the less appropriate certain items of clothing become. It is important to be aware of what looks good and keep to those items of clothing, rather than following fashion or trying to hold on to youth. For ladies, miniskirts may be an acceptable piece of clothing in your 20's, but not as appropriate in your 40's. A skirt just below the knee would seem more appropriate for the latter age bracket.

With regards to clothing, the difference between a fad and a fashion is the time component. A fad is short-lived, while a fashion endures.

"Fads are characterized by extreme enthusiasm for something that is shared by a large number of people over a relatively brief period." – *reference.com*

Fashion, on the other hand, is long-lived. However, I think style is what we should be aiming for, and our style, which can include fashion and fad but it is more than that.

"Fads are the kiss of death. When the fad goes away, you go with it." - *Conway Twitty*

In temperate regions, the year is divided into seasons: autumn, winter, spring and summer and as you know, each day has daytime and nighttime. These are all factors which should help you decide how to dress. Usually, each season or time of day has its own easily recognisable fashion, to aid a person in choosing what to wear. Avoid the tendency to be carried away by a certain style. Remember to choose carefully. For example, it is inappropriate to be dressed in sequins during the day.

Most places have a dress code, which may be written or unwritten. If an invitation card specifically states a particular dress code, do ensure you follow this. Most schools have a set uniform for the children, and the teachers should also dress appropriately, even if there is no written dress code. It would be very inappropriate for a female teacher to turn up at school wearing a miniskirt. Different places, e.g. churches, offices, restaurants, etc., have mainly unwritten dress codes.

When in doubt, the safest option would be to wear a plainer dress. It is always better by far to be under-dressed than overdressed. If you are unsure about a ball dress or dinner dress for an event, choose the safer option – the dinner dress. If you are invited to an event and the invitation does not specify the dress code, there is nothing wrong with asking the host.

Essential items for a lady's wardrobe:
- Little black dress – A black dress that will suit various occasions.
- A pair of tailored black trousers – Straight leg and flat front.
- A classic white shirt - It is wise to invest in at least 3 white shirts.
- A tea dress – Midi/knee-length dress; and not clingy.
- If you live in a temperate region invest in a warm winter coat/trench coat. In choosing a coat, choose a colour that will never look dated.
- Shoes – Invest in black medium-height pumps and ballet flats.
- A navy or black blazer – Invest in a good quality one that will last for years.
- Proper bras – Get properly fitted for a bra. A lot of women are known to wear the wrong size bra. Wearing the right bra can change the way the clothes look on you.
- Everyday quality classic leather bag – Start with black before buying other colours.
- Shawls/scarves – To keep warm or protect your dignity.

"I don't understand how a woman can leave the house without fixing herself up a little - if only out of politeness. And then, you never know, maybe that's the day she has a date with destiny. And it's best to be as pretty as possible for destiny." - Coco Chanel

Effortless Style

EFFORTLESS STYLE IS ABOUT looking stylish without it seeming like you made an effort. The concept of 'effortless style' can come across as a contradiction because being stylish does take an effort. However, over the years, one can learn to achieve the effortless look.

To achieve the effortless look, ensure that your clothes are comfortable, practical, and not fussy or garish. Keep it simple. When you decide to dress for the day, take into consideration the whole day ahead and what you are likely to be doing; that way, you can dress appropriately for the day. It is advisable for a lady not to wear heels if she is going to be out on a field all day.

The key is to know what style works best for your body type/shape and to recognise the colours that suit you.

"Fashion fades, only style remains the same." - *Coco Chanel*

Elegance

ELEGANCE IS DESCRIBED AS "being tasteful in dress, style, and design. It is also being dignified, graceful in appearance and behaviour, cleverly simple, and ingenious." - *freedictionary.com*

Elegance is both about appearance and attitude. An elegant lady, for example, stands out from the crowd, because she is not loud, does not talk at the top of her voice or screech, and can manage her moods. There is no public display of anger or emotion.

An elegant woman is always well turned out in appearance, clothing and personal grooming. She stands, talks and walks with confidence.

"Elegance does not consist of putting on a new dress." - Coco Chanel

Email Etiquette

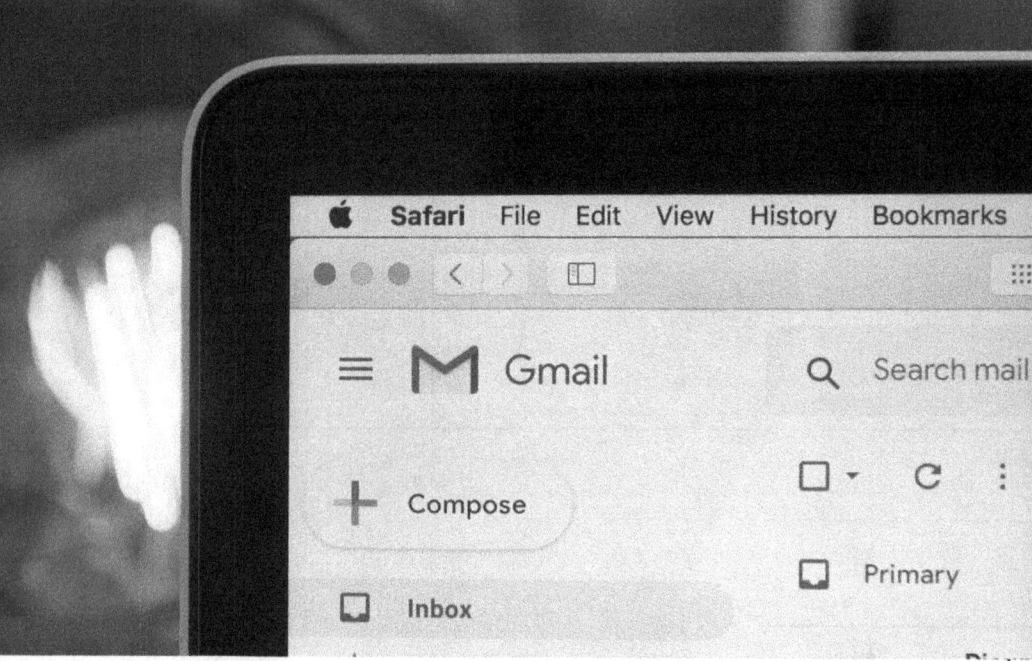

EMAILS ARE HOW MOST organisations, businesses and individuals communicate with each other via the internet. As such, it is very important to observe certain rules when sending emails. Remember that most, if not every email, sent via the internet are stored somewhere. Some companies also back up emails sent within their organisations.

Here are certain guidelines to observe when sending emails:
- Make sure you check spellings and use proper grammar and punctuation. Avoid using abbreviations.
- If sending emails to different people at the same time, make sure you blind carbon copy (bcc). Do not share someone's email

address without his or her consent.
- Keep emails brief, concise and to the point.
- Always try to respond to emails as soon as possible by the end of the business day. If you will not be able to deal with the email by the end of the day, try to acknowledge the email and let the sender know that you will get back to them.
- Avoid capitalising whole words or sentences (this is akin to shouting), and do not use fancy fonts.
- If you are sending a large attachment, zip or compress it.
- Always include a brief subject with your email.
- Never reply to an email when angry.
- Add disclaimers to business and office emails.
- Never forward junk mail or chain letters.

"Diamonds are forever. E-mail comes close." - *June Kronholz*

Entertaining Guests

AT SOME POINT IN our lives, we will have to entertain guests. For some, entertaining can be a breeze. However, for most, the thought of entertaining can be terrifying.

The key to successful entertaining is to ensure that your guests have a fabulous time and thoroughly enjoy themselves. Therefore, there are certain things to do to ensure that you host 'an event to remember':

- Prepare a guest list. Make sure the guests are people who are likely to get along with each other. Avoid inviting people who you know are not on speaking terms. For instance, it might not be a good idea to invite a couple who are separated or divorced and who are always arguing with one another.
- Prepare a menu. Unless you are a master chef, keep it simple. Think about your guests and try to remember their likes and

dislikes. If inviting people of different faiths, remember that there are certain foods that some faiths do not eat.
- Make sure your home is comfortable and clean. For example, you can light scented candles and if you wish, play good soft music (jazz - is a good example).
- Make sure you are dressed and ready before your guests arrive.
- Introduce guests to each other as they arrive and offer them drinks.
- See 'Dining Etiquette' for guidance on how to set a table.
- Do not allow a particular guest to monopolise you regarding conversation. As the host or hostess, your job is to mingle with all of the guests to make sure that they are ok.

"That's the secret of entertaining. You make your guests feel welcome and at home. If you do that honestly, the rest takes care of itself." - *Barbara Hall*

Fashion

THE FASHION INDUSTRY IS a multi-billion-pound industry with big designers, celebrities and buyers influencing the direction fashion goes. However, the final decision on the direction of fashion will ultimately depend on you, the final consumer, who will choose whether to buy into a trend or not.

The interesting thing to note about fashion is that it is important to develop your sense of style. Fashion should be a means of self-expression and an extension of your personality.

Do not be afraid to experiment with clothes and accessories, and be willing to mix and match your items. Fashion should be fun. When dressing up, have a focal point in mind; For ladies, it could be a big belt or a necklace. Pick one item that will stand out. Be careful not to over-accessorise.

> "Fashion has become a joke. The designers have forgotten that there are women inside the dresses. Most women dress for men and want to be admired. But they must also be able to move, to get into a car without bursting their seams! Clothes must have a natural shape." - *Coco Chanel*

Flatmates

UNLESS YOU ARE VERY wealthy, you may find that you have to share your living quarters with another person at some time in your life, i.e. a flatmate. Having to share a home with another person can turn out to be either a great experience or a complete nightmare. The key to having a wonderful experience is to establish ground rules from the start. Sharing a flat or house with someone means that there will be little privacy, except in your bedroom or the bathroom. You need to agree on boundaries. Certain key areas should be clarified:

- Friends: You need to discuss friends staying over or spending the weekend, etc. When someone starts to spend more than the occasional night, they are seen to be living on the property. It also means that the person is sharing electricity, food, water, the bathroom, etc.
- Clothes and belongings: Establish that there should be no sharing or taking of personal belongings without express permission.
- Food: Agree on how groceries should be shared, who cooks and when. If you cook, it is polite to offer your flatmate(s) some.
- Cleaning: It is best to have a rota for cleaning the flat or house and make sure the chores are shared out equally. If you can afford it, get a cleaner.

- Bills: Discuss how the bills will be divided and make sure that each person pays their fair share.
- Try to discuss all possibilities, e.g. talk about having parties, who will take the garbage out and when; whether it is acceptable to smoke in the home, etc.

The bottom line is, make an effort to get along with your flatmate(s), as this can be a wonderful experience.

"Everyone has this universal understanding of roommate drama."
- Leighton Meester

Fragrance

FRAGRANCE, ALSO KNOWN AS perfume or aftershave, was made only for close encounters. It should be subtle and not overpowering. People are not meant to be able to smell you a mile away before you ever get to them. If the fragrance you want to use is very strong, spray it in the air and walk through it.

Spray the fragrance on your pressure points, behind the ear, the wrist and inside of the elbow.

Heavy or strong fragrance should be used either in the cold months or in the evening. Summer/daytime perfumes should be light and airy.

"A woman's perfume tells more about her than her handwriting."
- Christian Dior

Friends

FRIENDS ARE AN ESSENTIAL PART of a person's life. It is important to be a good friend and also to have good friends. Your friends will enrich your life and will be part of it as you grow; at school, university, throughout your career, in business, and family life. Being a good friend and having good friends takes a lot of effort and patience; consider it a life-long investment. Like anything else in life, there is an element of risk involved. The key qualities that are important for being a good friend are:

- Loyalty.
- Trust.
- Unconditional love.
- Being able to share grief and sorrow: Be there for your friends and be a shoulder they can cry on.
- Generosity: Give them gifts to show you have thought about

them. If you cannot afford gifts, give them your time.
- Pure acceptance: Accept them for who they are and do not judge them.
- Laughter: Learn to laugh with your friends.
- Honesty and Openness.

"A friend is someone who understands your past, believes in your future, and accepts you just the way you are." *- Bernard Meltzer*

"A true friend is someone who thinks that you are a good egg even though he knows that you are slightly cracked." *- Bernard Meltzer*

Funerals
(See the section on 'Bereavement')

IF THERE IS ONE THING in life that is certain, it is death. At some point in our lives, we will have to attend a funeral. It is therefore important to know how to behave appropriately at funerals.
- Anyone can attend a funeral, except if the family has specifically asked for privacy.
- Concerning the appropriate attire for a funeral, black is not necessary anymore; any colour can be worn, although preferably not bright colours, unless specified. These days, some families will specify a colour, i.e. pink. Also, it is often no longer necessary to cover your hair for a funeral, although you may have to if you attend a Jewish or Greek orthodox funeral.
- Never out-do the chief mourner; always follow their lead.
- Make sure mobile phones are switched off and do not carry on a conversation while the service is taking place.

"It matters not how a man dies, but how he lives." *- Samuel Johnson*

Gifts – Giving and Receiving

OFTEN, WHEN WE WANT to show our appreciation to someone, we buy them gifts. We also give gifts for birthdays, weddings, etc. I believe that the best gifts, and the gifts that are usually well-received, are those that the receiver wants.

If giving gifts to someone you are close to, it is advisable to ask them if there is anything they want. When buying a gift for someone you are not close to, try to find out what they want from people who know them better. If you cannot afford what they want, buy them a gift voucher for the amount you can afford, preferably from a place that sells the gifts they want.

If you are unable to spend much money on a shop-bought gift for someone, a handmade gift can be a more economical alternative. Handmade gifts are often very much appreciated, as they are more personal and show that you have put in a lot of thought and effort. Some ideas for handmade gifts are:

- Handcrafted jewellery for ladies: You can buy cords, wires, packs of beads and charms to make your necklaces or bracelets.
- Knitted or crocheted garments or blankets: These are perfect gifts for the winter months if you are good at knitting or crocheting.
- Handmade candles: There are kits available that allow you to make candles of different shapes and scents. Most people love candles, as they complement the décor and create a warm ambience in any home.
- Homemade cakes, biscuits, and confectionary: These can make ideal gifts for those with a sweet tooth. Homemade jams, marmalades, and chutneys can also be a welcome gift.
- Personalised calendars: This is a particularly good idea for a Christmas gift, or a birthday gift towards the end of the year, with the New Year approaching. If you have a printer, you could print their favourite photos for each month of the year, and there will be plenty of calendar templates available online.
- Clay or pottery ornaments or hanging plaques: These can be decorated with meaningful quotes or special wordings for an even more personal touch.

YouTube is a fantastic place to find instructional videos and step-by-step guides if you are looking to create gifts.

"When I go to hell, I mean to carry a bribe: for look you, good gifts evermore make way for the worst persons." - *John Webster*

"Last year my boyfriend gave me a painting - a very personal one. I really prefer personal gifts or ones made by someone for me. Except diamonds. That's the exception to the rule." - *Minnie Driver*

Grace

WHILE WE MAY STRIVE to observe the rules of etiquette and social skills, we sometimes overlook another area that is equally important, i.e. the way we move and carry ourselves. This is sometimes known as deportment and is defined as "the manner in which a person behaves, especially in respect of physical bearing." – *freedictionary.com*

"Deportment is the way you express yourself through your features and by the way you move or hold your body. A woman who has beautiful deportment is said to be poised, graceful and elegant." – *Elegantwoman.org*. It is all to do with the way a lady carries herself, walks, sits and stands.

When you think - deportment, as an element of grace, poise, and class, who comes to your mind? For me personally, as a woman, it would be people like - Grace Kelly, Audrey Hepburn, and Diahann Carroll.

Regrettably, most of us learnt how to walk by copying imperfect and ungraceful models. It is also true that we have been marred by examples of bad walking from generation to generation.

How should we walk?

It should not be hasty, hurried, disjointed, nor aimless, but a deliberate rhythmical movement of the legs and feet in sync with gentle compensating movements of the head and arms in a slow, graceful swing.

The right posture is a delicate balance between a straight back, which is properly aligned with the head; the chin neither too low nor too high. The feet should be somewhat apart; the stomach should be in and shoulders held back and down, and the arms should be to the side. This posture is formed by training and exercise and is maintained by habit.

Sitting in Public

Legs also play an important role in your self-composure, poise, and confidence. Do not shake or jerk your legs constantly. Besides being an unwelcome distraction to others, it can look indecent. For ladies, the cardinal rule when sitting is to keep the knees together.

Learn how to place your hands properly either on the arms of the chair or on your lap. Relaxed hands give you an aura of serenity and poise.

How to Sit

"You should not fall into a chair or throw yourself on it, nor sit cautiously as though you suspect that it is dirty or would break under your weight.

Ladies should avoid sitting squarely on both feet, as that can appear too manly. Sit with your legs closed but lean them at an angle to one side.

Do not jump up or rise suddenly from your seat in an abrupt motion, nor lift your feet to 'stomp' as you get up." – Elegantwoman.org

> **"A graceful and pleasing figure is a perpetual letter of recommendation."** - *Francis Bacon, Sr.*

Gratitude

VOCABULARY.COM DEFINES GRATITUDE AS "a feeling of thankfulness and appreciation." It might seem like a small thing; however, it has the potential to make a huge impact. It is, therefore, a thing that should not be taken for granted.

Showing gratitude can be something as simple as saying thank you to someone for his or her help. It can be in the form of a hand-written note, a phone call, an email, a hug or a gift. The idea is to let the other person know that you appreciate whatever act of kindness may have been done. In expressing your gratitude, make sure it is sincere and not just empty words.

"Feeling gratitude and not expressing it is like wrapping a present and not giving it." - *William Arthur Ward*

"Gratitude is the most exquisite form of courtesy."
- *Jacques Maritain*

Grooming Regime

GROOMING IS DEFINED AS "to tend carefully as to person and dress; make neat or tidy or to make or keep (clothes, appearance, etc.) clean and tidy." – *dictionary.com*

A daily grooming regime should consist of:

- A proper bath or shower.
- Brushing of the teeth and, if necessary, using a mouthwash.
- Moisturising your skin, especially the face.
- Wearing deodorant and cologne/perfume.
- Wearing clean clothes, especially fresh underwear. Ladies may need to use a panty liner.
- Ensuring that hair is tidy, brushed or combed.

For ladies, the brows should be well-groomed and shaped. Aim for a natural look; over-plucked arches can create a disconcerting startled look.

Nails should be clean, shapely and of equal length. For ladies in particular, it is not advisable to wear nail art or nail jewellery. If you are not comfortable with long nails, it is advisable to keep them short and natural-looking.

It is also important to set time aside for yourself; shave, epilate or wax the hairs on your legs and armpits, pedicure, manicure, massage, and facial.

Ensure that shoes are clean and polished; do not wear shoes that are scuffed, especially heels.

To keep your skin looking healthy and well-nourished, drink plenty of water. Drinking water cleanses the body and re-hydrates the skin. Did you know that drinking at least two litres of water daily has been known to burn up calories?

'Grooming is the secret of real elegance. The best clothes, the most wonderful jewels, the most glamorous beauty don't count without good grooming." - *Christian Dior*

"You are your greatest asset. Put your time, effort and money into training, grooming, and encouraging your greatest asset."
- *Tom Hopkins*

H

Hair

HAIR LOOKS HEALTHIEST WHEN it is clean, smooth, lustrous, and free from dandruff and grease. For ladies, it is advisable to wash your hair at least once a week (depending on your hair type and race) and try to treat dandruff and other issues as soon as you notice them.

Stay away from complicated styles that are hard to maintain and try to avoid salons/hairstylists that only follow the styles that are in fashion. Regular trimming and cutting of hair will enable it to grow healthily.

- Avoid bad dye jobs. Colour should enhance and compliment your natural tones. Just because a colour looks good on someone else, does not mean it will suit your skin tone. It is best to have

your hair dyed professionally.
- If you have dyed hair, keep roots at bay and pay for regular maintenance.

Try to get your hair done professionally as often as possible. There is a tendency to damage your hair if you do it yourself all the time. The worst is when you apply a relaxer to your hair by yourself.

"No matter how chic your outfit is, bad nails or hair will ruin it all."
- Christy Buena

Handshakes

THE HANDSHAKE IS ONE of the oldest and most common customs for greeting people in most cultures. What we may not realise is that, when we shake hands with people, the handshake makes an impression. Deals are sealed with a handshake and wars may be averted with a handshake. We often see presidents and heads of state being photographed whilst shaking hands. This should tell us that handshakes are very important, and yet a lot of us underestimate the importance of this seemingly insignificant act.

However, it is important to note that this may not be the case in some cultures, and it is helpful if one can take time to learn about different ways of greeting in different cultures.

The following tips should be considered:
- Always use your right hand, and 'pump' the other person's hand two or three times before you let it go.
- Make sure that your fingers grip the other person's palm; this way you will not crush their fingers.
- Be careful not to clench the other person's hand in a bone-crushing grip, but do not offer a limp hand.
- Always check that your palms are not sweaty before shaking hands.

"More history is made by secret handshakes than by battles, bills, and proclamations." - *John Barth*

"Kind words, kind looks, kind acts and warm handshakes, these are means of grace when men in trouble are fighting their unseen battles." - *John Hall*

Hospitality

HOSPITALITY IS DEFINED AS "the friendly reception and treatment of guests or strangers, or the quality or disposition of receiving and treating guests and strangers in a warm, friendly, generous way." – *dictionary.com*

Being hospitable does not come naturally to everyone; some of us have to learn hospitality. But when you get it right, it can make a huge difference to your social life.

The key is to make people feel at ease when they are in your home. Do not make guests feel that they are putting you out; try to appear as though no extra effort has gone into having them.

"True hospitality consists of giving the best of yourself to your guests." - *Eleanor Roosevelt*

"Hospitality should have no other nature than love."
- *Henrietta Mears*

Houseguests

AT SOME POINT IN our life, we will be a houseguest or will have houseguests in our homes. However, not everyone is comfortable being a houseguest or having people in their homes. There are rules to observe:

- Take a gift for your host. It does not have to be anything expensive; it is the thought that counts.
- Be clean and tidy. Make sure your room is tidy. Clean the bathroom after using it. Clean up after you use the kitchen. Help around the house. Do not expect your host to wait on you hand and foot unless you cannot move.
- Do not be fussy about meals unless you are prepared to cook.
- Observe/learn the house rules. For example, in some homes, shoes are not permitted in the house (especially in Japanese homes).
- If you will be staying for a while, offer to help with the upkeep of the house.
- Do not invite guests into the home without letting your host know.

- Do not overstay your welcome.
- Leave a 'thank you' note when you leave.
- Lastly, if you have a houseguest in your home, be accommodating and tolerant. Hopefully, they will only be there for a short while.

"No guest is so welcome in a friend's house that he will not become a nuisance after three days." - *Titus Maccius Plautus*

"Nobody can be as agreeable as an uninvited guest." - *Kin Hubbard*

"The first day one is a guest, the second a burden, and the third a pest." - *Jean de la Bruyere*

Humour
(See the section on 'Jokes')

"Good humour is one of the preservatives of our peace and tranquillity." - *Thomas Jefferson*

"Laughter is the best medicine in the world." - *Milton Berle*

Integrity

INTEGRITY IS A WORD that is scarce nowadays. I often consider that it seems that very many people do not quite appreciate the meaning and importance of this very critical aspect of our character.

Integrity is defined in dictionary.com as "the adherence to moral and ethical principles; soundness of moral character; honesty." Another definition states that integrity is the "firm adherence to a code of especially moral or artistic values: incorruptibility." – *Merriam-Webster Dictionary*

Synonyms of integrity include honesty, truth, honour, reliability, and uprightness.

Integrity is about agreeing to do something and doing it, or showing up at an event when you say you will. These days, people feel that it is not a 'big deal' to say one thing and do another.

Integrity is about not letting people down, so you can look them in the eyes and hold your head high when you see them. It is about not disappointing that child you promised to take to the park or making sure that the report is ready when you said it would be. Integrity is about being a man or woman of your word.

> **"Simply let your 'Yes' be 'Yes,' and your 'No,' 'No'; anything beyond this comes from the evil one."**
> **- *Bible quote*** *(Matthew 5:37, New International Version)*

Interviews

BEING CALLED FOR AN interview signifies that you are one step closer to getting the job.

It implies that the company believes that you are qualified for the job. It would be a shame to be passed up for a position not for being unqualified, but because you messed up on interview etiquette. Here are some tips that might help you get that job:

- Turn up at least 15 minutes early. If it is a place you have never been to before, it is wise to do a dry run the day before. Familiarise yourself with the route.
- Make sure you dress appropriately for the interview. Women should make sure they do not wear anything clingy, revealing or too bright. Avoid fancy nails. Hair should be tidy and not distracting. Men should wear a suit and tie. If the company has a casual dress policy, make sure you err on the side of caution and be a little conservative. Though you may be aware the employees dress casually, do not turn up for the interview in

jeans, unless the company specifically states that you should. Shoes should be clean and polished
- Mobile phones and iPods must be turned off.
- When you walk into the room, give an appropriate greeting, i.e. "Good morning," or "Good afternoon," and avoid saying, "Hi". Shake hands with the person/people conducting the interview. See the section on 'Handshakes'.
- Maintain eye contact with the interviewer.
- Avoid fidgeting with your hands (keep them on your lap or at your sides), hair or clothing.
- When answering questions, be specific and do not exaggerate your skills. Try to speak with confidence. Do not use slang. You will likely be asked if you have any questions at the end of the interview. Your first question should not be, "How long before I get the job?" or "If I get the job, when will I get a pay rise?" Try to think of questions that will make you appear genuinely interested in the job. For example, "What challenges do you foresee in this job?"
- Do not go into an interview with too many bags. If you have to submit a paper or document during the interview, make sure you present it in a nice folder, so that it is not crumpled.

"I just think the word interview, although it is the view between two people exchanged, became a sort of cliché. You ask questions and the other one answers." - *Maximilian Schell*

**"I wish to Christ I could make up a really great lie. Sometimes, after an interview, I say to myself, 'Man, you were so honest - can't you have some fun? Can't you do some really down and dirty lying?' But the puritan in me thinks that if I tell a lie, I'll be punished."
- *Willem Dafoe***

Introductions

IMAGINE A SCENARIO WHERE you walk into a party with a friend. Your friend immediately spots someone she knows, and they start talking, not even acknowledging your presence. How would you feel? Most likely, you would feel ignored, awkward and unsure of what to do. If you are not the shy type, you may introduce yourself. However, if you are like most people, you will probably just walk away, hoping that you might find someone else that you know at the party.

We must learn how to make introductions so that people do not feel left out. If someone joins the group, introduce them immediately, so that they feel a part of the group and therefore feel invited to take part in the conversation.

When making introductions, remember that there is an appropriate order to do so: men should be introduced to women, juniors to elders and higher ranks. In a business setting, the client is usually considered a higher rank. In a formal gathering, it is best to use the first and last names, as well as any title, when making introductions.

It is better to say, "Allow me to introduce you to ….," rather than, "Let me introduce you to…," or "Please meet…". Alternatively, you could say, "I would like to introduce Ms …. from HR".

After the introduction, you may say, "It is nice to meet you," or "It is a pleasure to meet you". You can then follow with small talk.

In a formal setting, never say, "How are you doing?" or "What's up?"

Standing when being introduced is polite.

Introduce an individual to the group first and then the group to the individual. For example, "Mary, I would like to introduce Jim, Bob, and Sue. Everyone, this is Mary". Married couples should be introduced separately, although it is advisable to clarify the relationship, i.e. "and this is Sarah, Peter's wife".

> *"Do you suppose I could buy back my introduction to you?"*
> *- Groucho Marx*

Invitations (Sending/Receiving)

THROUGHOUT OUR LIFETIME, WE are bound to receive an invitation to one event or another, and also likely to have to send out invitations ourselves for occasions. There are numerous occasions/events in life that one might send or receive invitations for, and these can include: weddings, parties, christenings, Bat or Bar Mitzvahs, housewarming parties, fundraising events, birthdays, etc. It is best to get it right, whether sending out invitations or responding to one.

When sending out invitations to your guests, make sure that you include all of the following information:

- Your name/name of the host – Do not automatically assume that your guests will know who the invitation is from.
- Date of the event.
- Start time of the event.
- Location of the event – Include an address and postcode, so that it will be easier for guests to find the venue.
- Dress code – Let your guests know whether they should dress up or dress casually. If there is a theme, let your guests know what outfits they should wear.
- Contact number or email address – This is important so that your guests can RSVP. Make sure you include a date that your guests should RSVP by.

There is a simple rule when accepting or RSVPing to invitations; your response should be in the manner of the invitation. Always ensure you RSVP by the date stated on the invitation.

"The only man who is really free is the one who can turn down an invitation to dinner without giving an excuse." - *Jules Renard*

"I go where I'm invited. And all I can tell you is, if we accepted every invitation we had, I'd be away every day of my life."
- John Shelby Spong

Jabber

DICTIONARY.COM DEFINES THE WORD 'jabber' as "to talk or utter rapidly, indistinctly, incoherently, or nonsensically; chatter."

You would not want to be known as a 'jabberer'. When having a conversation, learn to speak slowly, particularly if you are aware that you usually talk fast. It also helps if you pronounce your words properly and clearly so that people can follow what you are saying.

When you speak rapidly or incoherently, people have to strain their ears to listen to you, and misunderstandings can occur if they are unable to follow what you are saying.

> **"When the eagles are silent the parrots begin to jabber."**
> *- Winston Churchill*

Jealousy

JEALOUSY IS SOMETIMES KNOWN as the green-eyed monster. This monster has been known to rear its ugly head in inappropriate situations.

The online Oxford Dictionary defines the word 'jealousy' as, "feeling or showing an envious resentment of someone or their achievements, possessions, or perceived advantages; Fiercely protective of one's rights or possessions."

The root of jealousy lies in a lack of contentment and a lack of love for people in general. Every human being is unique and, because we are all shaped by our various backgrounds and circumstances, we are bound to achieve things at different levels and at different times in our lives.

Learn to appreciate other people's gifts and talents and remember that you are a unique individual also created with gifts and talents.

> **"Jealousy is the greatest of all evils, and the one which arouses the least pity in the person who causes it."**
> *- François de la Rochefoucauld*

Jeans

JEANS ARE PROBABLY ONE of the most versatile items of clothing ever created. You can dress them up for a smart casual look, wear them for dress down days at work, or wear them just to relax on the weekend. However, whilst jeans are versatile, it does not mean that they suit every occasion.

I attended a wedding recently where one of the 'VIPs' wore jeans, and you should have seen the look of horror on the faces of the guests.

Jeans should not be worn to weddings, funerals or any formal event unless the invitation categorically states so. If you are not sure whether it is acceptable to wear jeans or not to an occasion, err on the side of caution and do not wear them.

"Jeans represent democracy in fashion." - *Giorgio Armani*

"I wish I had invented blue jeans. They have expression, modesty, sex appeal, simplicity - all I hope for in my clothes."
- *Yves Saint Laurent*

Jokes

THE THING TO REMEMBER about jokes is that not everyone shares the same sense of humour. What might be funny to you may not be funny to others, and some people might not consider your jokes or comments as being humorous. You should never try to impose your humour on others.

Be sensitive to other people's feelings and be careful not to offend with your jokes. There are wrong times and places for cracking jokes. For example, funerals are not the ideal place for jokes.

You should never crack jokes or make fun of people who are at their lowest. Also, be aware of people's sexuality, race, and religious beliefs.

Some people try to deal with life's issues by using humour; kindly bear with them. It may be their way of coping with life, e.g. bereavement.

Lastly, we should try to laugh at ourselves more often. Laughter is meant to be good for us; they say that laughter is the best medicine.

"In life there are always these things happening if you can just get the joke." - *Lynda Barry*

"It is the ability to take a joke, not make one, which proves you have a sense of humour." - *Max Eastman*

K

Kindness

KINDNESS IS THE PRACTICE of being or the tendency to be sympathetic and compassionate towards others. People go through a lot in life and because you have not 'walked in their shoes', it would be nice to always think about other people and to consider that there is always another side to every story or situation.

Kindness is expressed through consideration for others. In any social gathering, remember that kindness should supersede policies or protocols. Always act in a way that would not embarrass the other person, even if they do not observe etiquette themselves.

There are many ways in which we can show kindness. These might include:

- Giving a hug: This can be a comfort to the other person, especially if they are feeling upset.
- Smiling: People that smile often come across as more approachable and are usually perceived as being kind.
- Listening: Simply by listening to what another person has to say can mean a lot and may help them more than you realise.
- Showing empathy: This means showing understanding and being sympathetic to other people.
- Sharing and giving: Offering others your sweets etc., giving gifts or being charitable are all acts of kindness that will make others feel happy and will also make you feel good inside.
- Helping: When you offer to help someone, whether it is by giving someone a lift to an appointment or offering to do his or her grocery shopping, you will be making life easier for the other person, which is a valued act of kindness.

"A laugh, to be joyous, must flow from a joyous heart, for without kindness, there can be no true joy." - *Thomas Carlyle*

"A little thought and a little kindness are often worth more than a great deal of money." - *John Ruskin*

"Carry out a random act of kindness, with no expectation of reward, safe in the knowledge that one day someone might do the same for you." - *Princess Diana*

Kissing (Social Cheek Kissing)

CHEEK KISSING IS NOW something that is socially acceptable, and it is used to convey a greeting, thanks or appreciation. It is sometimes also used as a way of showing respect, regard or romantic interest.

When cheek kissing, start by offering your right cheek. Depending on the country and situation, the number of kisses can be either one, two, three or four. For example, in North America, the custom is usually one kiss on the cheek, while in Europe it can range from one to four kisses. In Belgium, three cheek kisses are customary, whereas it can be four in France, depending on the region.

As a general rule, avoid kissing strangers on the cheek. Do not kiss colleagues on the cheek, unless they offer you their cheek first. In business situations, avoid cheek kissing or any form of kissing. Kissing people who are family and close friends on the cheek is acceptable. If you are in doubt as to whether to cheek kiss or not, follow the lead of the other person.

Lastly, avoid air-kissing, as it makes you come across as insincere.

"People who throw kisses are mighty hopelessly lazy." - *Bob Hope*

Know-it-alls

WHO LIKES A 'KNOW IT ALL'? 'Know-it-alls' are people who give the impression that they have all the answers to every question; they usually scorn the advice, opinions, and suggestions of other people. Before you can speak, such people have already answered the question, and you never seem to be able to get a word in during a conversation, because they either know all the answers or disregard your opinion or suggestion. They always have a comment about everything and sometimes everyone.

In certain situations, it can be useful to have someone there that is knowledgeable. However, the rules of etiquette and social graces dictate that if you are a 'know-it-all', give other people a chance to voice their opinions or offer suggestions. Allow other people to speak, even if they might be wrong.

Besides, simply listening to what other people have to say may end up teaching you a thing or two.

In circumstances where you come across a 'know-it-all', please try to stay calm. It is advisable to just keep nodding until you can extricate yourself from the situation.

> **"The fellow who thinks he knows it all is especially annoying to those of us who do."** - *Harold Coffin*

> **"The only fool bigger than the person who knows it all is the person who argues with him."** - *Stanislaw Jerzy Lec*

Language

"THE METHOD OF HUMAN COMMUNICATION, either spoken or written, consisting of the use of words in a structured and conventional way." – *Oxford dictionary*

Language is also defined in the World Dictionary as "a system for the expression of thoughts, feelings, etc., by the use of spoken sounds or conventional symbols; the language of a particular nation or people, i.e. the French language; a particular manner or style of verbal expression."

Diverse language makes for a rich tapestry, and I believe that people should not only embrace the culture of other people, but they should also embrace their languages as well. This means accepting that not everyone will speak the same language as you.

Be tolerant of those who cannot speak your language; do not assume that other people speak and understand your language and then start chattering away to them in your native tongue. Just because someone may look like you or have a similar name, is no indication that you both speak the same language.

A word of caution! Do not automatically assume that someone does not understand your language and then talk negatively about them with the belief that they would not know what you are saying.

If travelling to a foreign country, attempt to learn a few words in the native language of that country (you can simply download translation apps such as Google translate). The local people will appreciate your efforts.

If you are in a business environment, speaking in a foreign language may make people feel uncomfortable, as they may assume that you are talking about them and that you do not want them to know what you are saying.

> "We all should know that diversity makes for a rich tapestry, and we must understand that all the threads of the tapestry are equal in value no matter what their colour." - *Maya Angelou*

Letter Writing (Handwritten Letters)

THE ART OF LETTER WRITING is one that is fast dying out in society today. With the advance of technology, emails, text and social media are the order of the day. People no longer take the time to sit down and handwrite letters, thank you notes or cards.

There is a certain joy that I feel whenever I receive handwritten letters or notes.

Nowadays, handwritten letters are usually informal and only written to family members or friends.

If it is a formal letter, it usually should be typed and it should consist of:

- Your address in the upper right-hand corner.
- The date - a few lines under your address (preferably write the date in full, i.e. 20th September 2019).
- Recipient's address should be slightly lower down than your address, but to the left of the letter.
- Salutation, i.e. "Dear Mr or Mrs (Surname) Full name or "Dear Sir or Madam", written on the left, a couple of lines under the recipient's address.
- Contents of your letter should be well structured, clear and concise.
- Closing - i.e. "Yours faithfully" (if you have used Sir or Madam as your salutation) or "Yours sincerely" (if you have used the recipient's name as the salutation).
- Your signature.

An informal letter, on the other hand, does not need to be as structured, but in general, the following should be included:

- Your address in the upper right-hand corner, so that the recipient knows where to send their reply.
- Date, which usually goes under your address.
- Salutation, i.e. "Dear John" – It is not necessary to write their full name.
- Closing, i.e. "Best wishes. Warm regards, thank you."
- Your name.

"Once in a while you start having second thoughts, then you read a letter from someone that lifts your spirits so much - it really makes a huge difference. I love reading them." - *Corbin Bleu*

Love

LOVE IS NOT SIMPLY an emotion as some would like to think. On the contrary, love is a choice. Love is a decision that you make in life. You decide whether to love someone, regardless of whether the feelings are reciprocated.

The best way to show love is to treat people the way they want to be treated and not necessarily how you think they should be treated. Take time to find out about the person and find out about their likes and dislikes.

Love makes the world go around!

"Love is always bestowed as a gift - freely, willingly and without expectation. We don't love to be loved; we love to love."
- *Leo Buscaglia*

"Love never gives up. Love cares more for others than for self. Love doesn't want what it doesn't have. Love doesn't strut."
- *Bible quote* *(1 Corinthians 13:4, The Message)*

Make-up

CONCERNING MAKE-UP FOR WOMEN, always consider that less is more, especially for the daytime. You do not need to be made up 24/7.

During the daytime, you should only wear as much make-up as is needed. Work at the **'no-make-up' look, instead of the 'made-up' look**. Bad make-up can be worse than no make-up, while too much make-up can often be seen as bad make-up.

If you can, it is worth visiting a cosmetic stand in a department store and asking a professional to show you the best way to apply make-up; you do not have to buy their products after the make-up session, no matter how much pressure they may put on you. This is perfectly acceptable to Department stores.

Avoid applying your make-up in public, for example on the train or bus. It makes others feel uncomfortable and unwillingly draws attention to you.

"Whether you are sixteen or over sixty, remember; understatement is the rule of a fine makeup artist." - *Helena Rubinstein*

"The most beautiful makeup of a woman is passion. But cosmetics are easier to buy." - *Yves Saint-Laurent*

Manners

"A WAY OF DOING, being done, or happening; mode of action, occurrence; also, ways of behaving with reference to polite standards; social comportment." – *dictionaryreference.com*

Without even realising it, we use manners every day. Generally, they are good manners, yet other times our manners can be questionable.

From a very young age, even before we could speak properly, most of us were taught to say 'please', 'thank you', etc. Later on, as we grew older, we learned other everyday words and phrases, like 'excuse me', 'I am sorry', etc.

Other forms of good manners include: holding the door open for someone, offering your seat to an elderly or infirm person, returning phone calls promptly, RSVPing to an invitation, or sending out thank you cards, etc.

Most of the rules of etiquette will fall under manners because it is about showing respect and consideration for others.

"Good manners will often take people where neither money nor education will take them." - *Fanny Jackson-Coppin*

"Manners maketh a man." - *William Horman*

Mind Your Language
(See the section on 'Language')

LANGUAGE CONSISTS OF WORDS used to communicate and express ourselves.

In this new age of political correctness, our choice of words needs to be carefully selected. Certain words can be misconstrued if not used correctly or in the right context. Various words cannot be used regarding different social groups, etc. For example, it is no longer appropriate to use the term 'old people'; the correct term is 'senior citizens'.

"When people talk about political correctness, the only element of any value is good manners." - *Paul Johnson*

Neighbours

UNLESS YOU PLAN ON living on a 'desert island', you are more likely to have neighbors wherever you live (except you live in a very remote area by yourself). There are interesting quotes from the bible that instruct us to "love our neighbors the way we love ourselves" (Matthew 22: 39; NLT version) and to "treat others the way we would want to be treated ourselves." (Luke 6: 31; TPT version)

We should, therefore, have consideration and respect for our neighbours. Consideration means being mindful of others, being thoughtful, and being sympathetic. If you know that your actions will cause strife between your neighbour and yourself, avoid carrying out those actions. To put it simply, refrain from actions that may likely upset your neighbours. On the other hand, it is good practice to discuss such actions/events with your neighbour before you do them. For example:

- Do not park in their driveway or allow your guests to park there.
- If you share a communal corridor, do not leave your belongings in the corridor and always try to keep the area clean and tidy.
- If you have pets, do not allow your pets to wander into your neighbors' garden, and if they do, apologise immediately and make sure you clean up any mess.
- If you intend to have a party, inform your neighbours before the occasion, and you may also invite them to the party.
- Be a good neighbour by being willing to accept parcels for your neighbors when they are out. Also, if their mail is mistakenly dropped through your letterbox, take it around and put it through their letterbox.
- Do not play music so loud as to disturb your neighbour's peace.
- Look out for your neighbours, especially those that are elderly or infirm, and those who may be on their own and lonely.

Remember, etiquette is about having consideration and respect for others.

"Good fences make good neighbours." - *Robert Frost*

No

IS IT OKAY TO say 'No'? The simple answer is Yes! It is perfectly acceptable to say 'No' sometimes. We live in a world where we try to please others, often to the detriment of ourselves. Some people over-commit to things and then become overwhelmed. If you know that you are unable to do what is asked of you, it is okay to politely decline from the outset. In certain situations, you may have to explain why you have to turn down a request, an invitation etc.; other times you need not offer any such explanation if you do not have a close relationship with the person.

If asked to do something which you are unable to do, you can simply thank the person for asking you and politely decline, i.e. "Thank you for asking me; although it is an honour, I will have to decline at this time, because I simply cannot commit due to my work schedule."

Try saying 'No' a few times and you will get a sense of liberation. The question you should ask yourself is this; what is the worst thing that can happen if I say 'No'?

"You just have to do your own thing, no matter what anyone says. It's your life." - *Ethan Embry*

Notes

WHEN WAS THE LAST time you picked up your pen to scribble a note to someone? Like handwritten letters, sending notes is also a dying act. Most people do not even send cards anymore; I know this because one of the major card companies recently went into administration.

When you send a card/note to someone, it shows that you care; that you were thinking of them and you went out of your way to pick a card or write a note to them. Receiving a handwritten note can seem warmer and more heartfelt than receiving a message sent over the Internet. I always appreciate handwritten notes.

It is also polite to send a 'thank you' note to someone who has invited you to a party or event, or when you are sent a gift and do not get the chance to say 'thank you' in person.

"When your heart speaks, take good notes." - *Judith Campbell*

Office Etiquette

THERE IS A PROPER manner in which one should conduct oneself in an office environment. It is not just about how you conduct yourself within the office environment, but also about representing the company wherever you are.

In the office, your colleagues should be treated with courtesy and respect. This means that you should be aware of the volume of your voice when speaking, either on the phone or to someone else, especially in an open-plan office.

If you have to eat within the office or in the staff room, make sure that your food is not likely to smell strong and offend people. If you have a staff kitchen, keep it tidy and wash up after yourself.

Never borrow items without asking for permission, and if possible, do not borrow at all.

Do not gossip about your colleagues. Every office environment has a culture; learn about your office culture.

Lastly, most offices have a dress code; always adhere to the code. It is unbecoming to show off body parts, e.g. midriff, etc., in an office environment.

"Good manners are cost-effective. They not only increase the quality of life in the workplace, they contribute to employee morale, embellish the company image, and play a major role in generating profit." - *Letitia Baldrige*

Order/Organised

WHILE THESE TWO WORDS can sometimes be defined differently, they have enough similar meanings that help to convey the message and allow one to discuss them together.

There is nothing as chaotic as a disorderly life.

Order is: "the arrangement or disposition of people or things in relation to each other according to a particular sequence, pattern, or method" - *dictionary.com*

When things are organised and arranged in an orderly way, life is made much simpler. One can find things if and when needed and time is managed effectively. Conversely, when there is disorder, precious time is wasted either looking for things or trying to arrange things.

Being disorganised and messy could also send the wrong message to others that you are not in control of your life and could not be trusted to handle responsibilities effectively. I am sure we can all recall one person in our lives who constantly uses the phrase "Excuse the mess, but I know where everything is!"

Organised is defined – particularly in the transitive verb, as: "to arrange by systematic planning and united effort." – *Merriam-Webster dictionary*; and: "to arrange or prepare (something), usually requiring time or effort." – *thefreedictionary.com*

It does pay to have an organised life both at home and in the workplace. Being organised makes your life and that of everyone around you easier. It has been proven that people who are organised are more productive, as they spend less time trying to sort out the chaos.

When organising yourself, start by putting things in order of priority, i.e. urgent, important, less significant, etc. It is also a good idea to file paperwork, e.g. letters and bills in labelled files to make them easy to find. It is advisable to keep a diary or appointment book and set reminders for yourself, to avoid missing appointments.

"Chaos was the law of nature; Order was the dream of man."
- *Henry Adams*

"Have a time and place for everything, and do everything in its time and place, and you will not only accomplish more, but have far more leisure than those who are always hurrying." - *Tryon Edwards*

"Organizing is what you do before you do something, so that when you do it, it's not all mixed up." - *A.A. Milne*

Original

SOMETHING IS REFRESHING ABOUT being original and being true to oneself. Do not compare yourself to others and do not copy others. You might find that even the people you copy are not sure of who they are. Be creative and innovative; it will get you further in life than being a copy.

"You were born an original; do not die a copy." - *John Mason*

"Always be a first-rate version of yourself, instead of a second-rate version of somebody else." - *Judy Garland*

"Remember always that you have not only the right to be an individual; you have an obligation to be one. You cannot make any useful contribution in life unless you do this." - *Eleanor Roosevelt*

P

Patience

PATIENCE! PATIENCE!! PATIENCE!!! Patience is said to be a virtue. We have to learn to be tolerant of other people and to be more accommodating; because we all come from different backgrounds and are shaped by different situations, experiences and circumstances.

In life, we sometimes have to wait for things to happen. For example; waiting in line at the supermarket or sometimes being patient with people who do not move at the pace you would like them to.

When you have mastered the skill of being patient, it can help you to avoid arguments in any social situation. Even when you vehemently disagree with someone, you should know instinctively when to get into an argument and when not to.

"Forgive, forget. Bear with the faults of others, as you would have them bear with yours. Be patient and understanding. Life is too short to be vengeful or malicious." - Phillip Brooks

"To disagree, one doesn't have to be disagreeable."
- Barry M. Goldwater

Perfume
(See the section on 'Fragrance')

"A woman who doesn't wear perfume has no future." - Coco Chanel

Please

IT MAY SEEM LIKE a very simple word, yet it can make such a huge difference in human interactions. Learning to say 'please' is just simple courtesy. Saying 'please' shows that you have respect, consideration and regard for the other person. Saying please to waiters, colleagues and even people younger than yourself also shows that the individual was brought up with good manners.

> **"Learning to say 'please', 'thank you' and 'I'm sorry', will make the world go round."** - *Olu Adeaga*

Punctuality

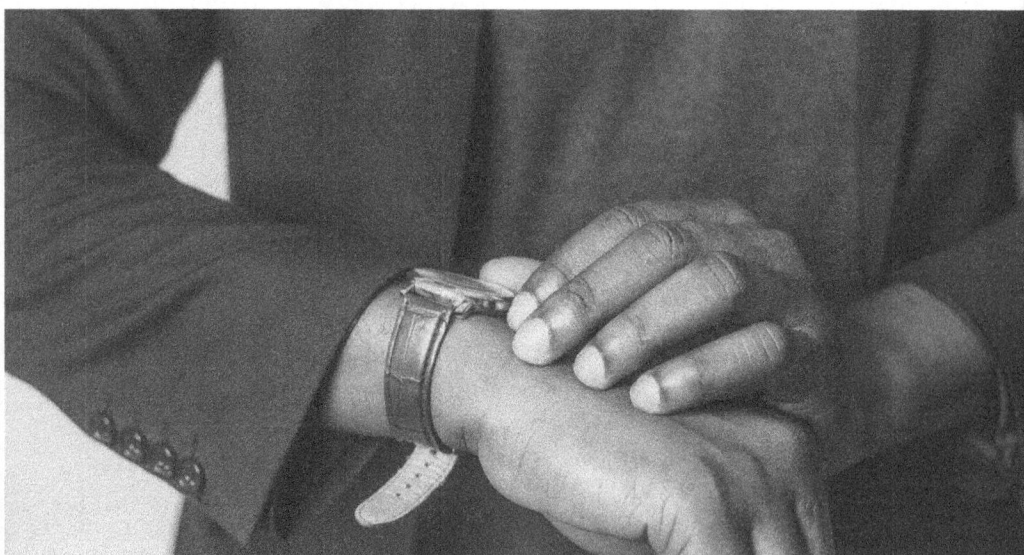

ARRIVING LATE FOR A MEETING, event, etc., is simply a sign of dishonour and disrespect.

A key reflection of the value we place on people is the 'ability' and the effort we make to respect and value their time. Valuing people is simply considering others when a meeting or appointment is set. That being said, you do what is necessary to ensure you arrive in good time. This is so that you do not keep someone else waiting for no good reason. It shows both self-respect and respect for others when you value them by valuing their time.

The excuse given by most people when they turn up late for an event or meeting is that they were held up by traffic or delays on public transportation. While the occurrence of this is fully appreciated, it is a fact of life and hence no longer an excuse. The trick is to always build in extra time and never assume that the roads will always be free of traffic or that public transportation will run smoothly. It is far better to get to a meeting early than late. If you arrive at an important meeting at least ten minutes beforehand, it shows that you are serious about the business.

Furthermore, there is no excuse for being late, since most adults know how long it takes to get dressed, have breakfast and find their way around their community.

It is rude to be late – it is disrespectful to use the age-old excuse of, "You know me; I have never been known to arrive on time."

If you know that you are going to be unavoidably late, it is common courtesy to make a phone call or send a message to let the other party know that you are running behind and with a clear idea of when you should be expected to arrive.

If you have called a meeting, honour people by showing up on time and starting the meeting on time.

Lastly, if you do turn up late, make sure you apologise, even if you have already sent a message to say that you were running late.

> **"Better three hours too soon, than one minute too late."**
> *- William Shakespeare*

Quality

IT IS A KNOWN fact that quality is better than quantity. A clear example is that of cheap products, especially clothes. Whilst, not all-cheap clothing are of poor quality, some items are noticeably so. In the long run, it is more cost-effective to spend more money buying a good quality leather bag, for example, than buying a cheap synthetic leather-look bag that you will have to replace every six months.

> "You can't fake quality any more than you can fake a good meal."
> - *William S. Burroughs*

Quarrels

THE FREE DICTIONARY DEFINES a quarrel as: "An angry disagreement; argument: A cause of disagreement or dispute; grievance."

Even in the most solid of relationships, it is not unusual for quarrelling to sometimes happen, i.e. between husbands and wives, siblings, best friends and colleagues. The definition states that quarrels usually occur because of a disagreement. The thing to note, however, is that, just because you disagree with someone's opinion, suggestion, etc., does not mean you have to quarrel. Remember, everyone is entitled to his or her opinion, and we all see things from our perspective.

Always try to reach a compromise when there is a disagreement. Agree to respect the other person's point of view. You are under no obligation to accept it, but just acknowledge that it is how they see things.

> **"Where do you think all these appalling wars and quarrels come from? Do you think they just happen? Think again. They come about because you want your own way, and fight for it deep inside yourselves. You lust for what you don't have and are willing to kill to get it. You want what isn't yours and will risk violence to get your hands on it."** - ***Bible quote*** *(James 4:1, The Message)*

Queuing/Queue Jumping

IF YOU HAPPEN TO have observed people living in the United Kingdom, for example, you would be aware that the British are known for queuing. It is a known fact that a 'Brit' will join a queue first and then ask what the queue is for later.

Most of us hate standing in queues. However, we will most likely have to join a queue, even if it is a short one, during any given day or time.

Some important points to note are:
- Be patient.
- If you are in a queue to pay for something, make sure you have your preferred method of payment ready by the time you get to

the front of the queue.

- Do not invite your friend, who you have just noticed is at the end of the queue, to come and join you in front. Remember that other people were there before your friend.
- Do not ask the person in front or behind you to keep your place whilst you go off to get a couple of items you forgot. It is considered to be cheeky.
- Try to respect people's personal space. Do not stand too close to the person in front or behind you in a queue.
- On a positive note, you can say hello or chat with the person in front or behind you. I know a couple that met in a queue and they are now married. You just never know who is standing behind or in front of you; it may be your date with destiny.
- The number one faux pas you can commit about queues is queue jumping. Wait patiently in line and wait your turn.

"An Englishman, even if he is alone, forms an orderly queue of one."
- *George Mikes*

Respect/Regard

SOME OF THE VARIOUS definitions of the word 'regard' are: "To look at attentively; observe closely; To think of or consider in a particular way; Respect, affection, or esteem; To relate or refer to; concern; careful thought or attention." - *thefreedictinary.com*

When you show someone regard, you are showing respect for that person. As mentioned, a few times already, but worth emphasising now and again, social etiquette is all about showing consideration and respect for others.

There are countless ways to show respect and regard for other people, and listed below are just a few of the more customary manners:

- Correctly addressing the other person. For example, you could address your clients or customers as 'Sir' or 'Madam'.
- Avoiding swearing and using foul language.
- Having good manners, i.e. saying, 'Please' and 'Thank you'.
- Holding a door open for someone who is behind you.
- Pulling out a chair for another person to sit on.
- Listening while others are talking and not talking over them.
- Taking care of other people's belongings. If someone has lent you something, make sure you look after that item and return it in the same condition in which it was lent to you.
- Being sincere and trustworthy.
- Giving compliments and showing gratitude when other people help you or do something nice for you.

"Respect is how to treat everyone, not just those you want to impress." - *Richard Branson*

Restaurants

IF YOU PLAN TO go to a restaurant, it is best to plan by booking a table. Doing so, ensures you avoid the embarrassment of getting to the location only to find out that it is fully booked. When you arrive at the restaurant, if you are uncomfortable with the table you are assigned, ask politely to be moved to another table. If the restaurant is unable to accommodate your request, especially on a busy night, do not make a fuss.

Try to place your order as soon as possible. If you are part of a group, it is best to share dishes. Please note that, if you are not the one paying the bill, be modest in your choice of food. Do not be tempted to order the most expensive dish on the menu. If you are part of a group, wait patiently for all the others to be served before you start to eat. If your dish is taking longer than necessary, you may ask the others to go ahead. (*See the section on 'Dining Etiquette'*)

Remember to show respect and regard to your waiter(s), and remember to say please and thank you as they serve you. It also helps to smile.

If you are not happy with your food, there is a proper way to complain. (See the section on 'Complaints')

Remember to tip the waiter/waitress at the end of the evening. (See the section on 'Tipping')

"Life is like a restaurant; you can have anything you want as long as you are willing to pay the price." - *Moffat Machingura*

"When you go to a restaurant, the less you know about what happens in the kitchen, the more you enjoy your meal."
- *Jeffrey Wright*

Restroom

'LEAVE IT AS YOU would like to find it', is the golden rule where restrooms (or loos, toilets, etc.) are concerned.
- Always knock on a toilet door before you enter; some doors have been known to have faulty locks, and you could end up embarrassing someone.
- Wipe the toilet seat after you have used it.
- Flush the toilet and preferably close the lid before flushing.
- Wash your hands after using the toilet.
- Wipe the sink area after use.
- If after use you are aware the toilet roll has run out, warn the next person before they use it.
- If you comb your hair in the restroom, make sure you do not leave hair in the sink. The same rule applies for make-up; do not leave any make-up residue in the sink.

- Toilet paper should not be left on the floor; kindly put these in the bin.
- Avoid leaving toilet rolls on the floor of the toilet. It is more hygienic to place them on/in a holder or on a countertop.
- Sanitary towels etc. should be put in the designated bin. Most importantly, they should not be flushed down the toilet.
- If there is a problem with the restroom, make sure you report it as soon as possible.

"Why do they call it the restroom? Is there anybody just resting in this room?" - Dane Cook

"I listen like mad to any conversation taking place next to me just trying to hear why this is funny. Women's restrooms are especially great. I wash my hands twice waiting for people to come in and start talking." - Lynda Barry

Riches

WHEN OUT SOCIALLY, NEVER flaunt wealth. It is a well-known fact that the people who are really wealthy never flaunt their wealth. Most sophisticated families never talk about how much money they earn, how much they have, or how rich they are. If you find yourself to be a newly wealthy person, do not become a snob and turn your back on your friends. There is joy in giving and sharing the wealth. It is a thoughtful gesture to make donations to charities or to give to those that are genuinely in need.

> "... anyone can acquire wealth; the real art is giving it away."
> - *Daisy Goodwin*

> "The things we feel deeply are the things that make us rich."
> - *Marty Rubin*

Sales

WE ALL LOVE SALES! Who doesn't love to find items reduced by 50% or more? It is amusing to hear the way people plan for 'the sales'. I have a friend who will stay in a queue as early as 5 am, just to be one of the first to get into her favourite shops during their sales.

Please note that just because something is on sale does not mean that you should buy it. Buy it only if you need it.

Some rules for the sales:

- To make the most of a sale, especially if there are specific items that you want, go to the store and try out the items before the sale starts. Try the size and choose the colour(s) you want.
- Try on the clothes so you do not have to return them.

- If there is a mad rush during the sales, do not snatch items out of another shoppers' hands. It is advisable to keep a close watch on the shopper, so you can be in the best position to pick up the item whenever they decide to put it down. However, be discreet about this action as it may be discomfiting for other shoppers if they feel you are 'stalking' them.
- Only buy what you need. Just because something is on sale does not mean that it is a good investment.
- It is important to find out about the store's return/exchange and refund policy.
- Sales are opportunities to invest in quality and classic items that will last you for years.
- In temperate regions, certain items, such as winter clothing, maybe cheaper during the summer sales.
- It may seem obvious, but wear comfortable shoes.
- If you have been walking around all day, do not try on shoes, because your feet are likely to be swollen and there is the likelihood that you will buy the wrong size. (That is why it is best to try on the shoes beforehand.
- Do not try on shoes in a store when you have smelly feet. This potentially leaves an odour in the shoe and can be quite disconcerting for the next customer who wants to try then on. Always ask for a pair of socks from the sales rep (most stores carry this item to use when trying on shoes.)

"There is a difference between what you want, and what you need."
- Abhijit Naskar

Sincerity

THE WORD 'SINCERE' IS defined in dictionary.com as follows: "free of deceit, hypocrisy, or falseness; earnest: Genuine; real; a sincere friend:

Pure; unmixed; unadulterated".

To be trusted and respected by others, it is important to be sincere.

> **"The most exhausting thing in life is being insincere."**
> *- Anne Morrow Lindbergh*

Smile

SMILING IS A SOCIAL skill that is so often overlooked and underestimated, yet it is one of the most powerful tools available to us as human beings in social situations. A genuine smile makes people feel comfortable around you. When you smile, people see you as someone approachable, warm, friendly and open.

A smiley, friendly face can make people more attracted to you.

I love the quotes below:

"There are hundreds of languages in the world, but a smile speaks them all." - *Unknown*

"Every time you smile at someone, it is an action of love, a gift to that person, a beautiful thing." - *Mother Theresa*

"Too often we underestimate the power of a touch, a smile, a kind word, a listening ear, an honest compliment, or the smallest act of caring, all of which have the potential to turn a life around."
- *Leo Buscaglia*

Spaghetti

IT IS WIDELY BELIEVED that Marco Polo introduced spaghetti to Italy after his visit to China. The Chinese are thought to have been making noodles made from rice flour for years, whereas the Italians make spaghetti from wheat flour.

What is the correct way to eat spaghetti, you ask? Is it with a spoon and fork or simply with a fork?

Please note that Italians, in general, do not use a spoon to eat their spaghetti; they only use a fork, and that is why they mainly serve spaghetti in a bowl and not on a flat plate.

However, most restaurants will place a spoon and fork beside your spaghetti dish. To correctly eat spaghetti with a spoon and fork, pick up the spaghetti with the tines of your fork, hold the spoon in your left hand, twirl the fork into the bowl of the spoon until the spaghetti is completely wrapped around the fork, then lift the fork to your mouth.

"Spaghetti can be eaten most successfully if you inhale it like a vacuum cleaner." - *Sophia Loren*

T

Table Setting
(See the section on 'Dining Etiquette')

Texting

TEXTING IS ALSO KNOWN as SMS, which stands for 'Short Message Service.' Therefore, the first thing to note is that text messages should not be long. The basic rule is to keep them as short as possible.

- Be lively with conversations. Do not just send 'k' for 'okay'.
- Double-check the mobile number and message before you send it. Once it is sent, it cannot be unsent.
- Do not assume that everyone has stored your number on his or her phone. Make sure to add your name when sending text

messages, except if the message is to close family members or friends who you know have your number.
- Do not send messages late at night; it is disturbing.
- Avoid sending sad or bad news by SMS. It is in bad taste.
- Do not send text messages whilst driving. I am sure you know that it is dangerous and against the law in most countries.

"The interesting thing about text is that, as a medium, it separates you from the person you are speaking with, so you can act differently from how you would in person or even on the phone."
- Aziz Ansari

"Today's kids aren't taking up arms against their parents; they're too busy texting them." *- Nancy Gibbs*

Thank you – The simple act of showing gratitude
(See the sections on 'Appreciation' and 'Gratitude')

SAYING 'THANK YOU' AFTER someone has shown you an act of kindness is never too difficult. However, in a culture where many people feel that the world owes them a living, this act is being lost. When people receive things now, they often consider it a 'right' and forget to say 'thank you'.

A 'thank you' lets people know that you appreciate whatever it is that the other party has done. When you say thank you, it encourages people to do more for you.

Make it a habit to thank people, regardless of their status in life; thank your friends, colleagues and family. No man is an island; we are who we are because of the efforts of different people.

> "Saying thank you is more than good manners. It is good spirituality." - *Alfred Painter*

Tipping

WHEN YOU DINE AT a restaurant, endeavour to tip the waiter or waitress (unless the service has been appalling). Tipping is just a way to show that you appreciate the service that you have received. The amount/percentage you should give differs from country to country; however, it usually ranges from 10% to 20%. If someone goes above and beyond what they are supposed to do, it is a good idea to give more to show your appreciation. In America, most people tip 15% - 20%, whilst in the UK, it is 10% rising to 15% if you have received exceptional service. In some parts of France, it is between 5% to 15%.

Most restaurants now add a service charge or gratuity to the bill and you, therefore, are not obliged to give a tip (except you wish to appreciate an exceptional service).

In America, it is customary to tip almost everybody, e.g. your hairdresser, taxi driver, doorman, cleaner, nanny, the housekeeper at the hotel, etc.

Please note that in some countries it is considered an insult to tip, so it is important to read up on the culture of a place before you visit.

"Know how and how much to tip people who expect gratuities, even in the case of poor service." - *Marilyn vos Savant*

"When you tip your server well, you're spreading goodwill and love." - *Bert McCoy*

Tolerance
(See the section on 'Patience').

BEING TOLERANT MEANS YOU accept that other people are entitled to their customs, opinions and beliefs and that they do not always have to see things from your point of view. We are all shaped differently by our backgrounds and circumstances, and this can often cloud our worldview.

Be willing to accept different views, be open-minded, be more understanding, and charitable.

"In a multi-racial society, trust, understanding and tolerance are the cornerstones of peace and order." - *Kamisese Mara*

"It is thus tolerance that is the source of peace, and intolerance that is the source of disorder and squabbling." - *Pierre Bayle*

Travel

TO GET THE MOST out of your travel experiences, be a well-mannered traveller:
- Learn the customs of the country you are travelling to. If you

do this, then you are more likely to understand the locals and less likely to spend time complaining about how they behave or do things.
- Respect their customs and traditions.
- Be courteous to people. If you do not understand their language, get or find an interpreter. I have found that one language that almost everyone understands is a smile.
- Whatever country you are in, a smile will always let people know that you are friendly and approachable. A smile will usually diffuse any social tension or awkwardness.
- Be patient. In some countries, things may be done at a slower pace than in your native country.

"Perhaps travel cannot prevent bigotry, but by demonstrating that all peoples cry, laugh, eat, worry, and die, it can introduce the idea that if we try and understand each other, we may even become friends." - *Maya Angelou*

Trust

TRUST IS DEFINED AS "reliance on the integrity, strength, ability, surety, etc., of a person or thing; confidence. Also, confidence in and reliance on good qualities, especially fairness, truth, honour, or ability."
- *dictionary.com*

Trust is a two-way street; you have to learn to trust people (despite the experiences you may have had in the past), and also you should be someone who people can trust, i.e. a trustworthy person who can be relied on.

As discussed earlier, under the 'Integrity' section, there is something to be said about being acknowledged as a woman or man of integrity. Be known as a person whose 'yes' means 'yes', and whose 'no' means just that. Remember - Integrity engenders trust whilst a lack of it destroys trust.

"Trust is like a vase...once it's broken, though it can be fixed the vase will never be the same." - *Carol Brady*

Unappreciated

THE TERM 'UNAPPRECIATED' IS defined as: "not given or shown thanks or gratitude."- *collinsdictionary.com*. Everyone wants to feel appreciated and respected. Ensure that you remember to say thank you to someone if they go out of their way to help you.

> **"A lack of appreciation and respect can be a sad end to many wonderful relationships."** - *Bernajoy Vaal*

Unapproachable

OUR BODY COMMUNICATES OUR feelings and emotions, even when we are not speaking. Sometimes, you come across people who look unfriendly and unapproachable. Such people may have a scowl on their faces or a stern look (sometimes unknown to them). Unfortunately, and often unintentionally, they do not realise that their body language and posture are screaming: "Do not come near me". More often than not, such people may not necessarily be unfriendly and it could quite simply be that they are just shy, reserved or uncomfortable.

However, if over the years you have been told that you seem unapproachable, then it is your responsibility to do something about it. You might need to make an effort to smile more or change the way you stand, i.e. standing without folding arms in a combative posture. Many people fold their arms out of habit, but this body language can be interpreted as: 'Proceed with caution, I am not in the mood for socialising".

"Sometimes it is better to show our vulnerability/pain/regrets so others don't think us impervious/unapproachable - be real/open."
- Jay Woodman

Underwear

THERE IS A REASON it is known as 'underwear'; it is not meant to be seen and was designed to be worn under clothes. We are not meant to see the colour, fabric or design of your underwear.

For ladies, Bras or straps should not be seen through a sheer blouse. Should you need to wear a sheer top, it is advisable to wear a nude-coloured camisole underneath. The same rule applies to sheer dresses.

White trousers worn with thongs or coloured panties underneath do not look classy. Ensure you wear nude-coloured underwear with white trousers. White on white does not work. Even when you wear nude panties, it is not a good look when the panty line is visible. It is a good idea to invest in seamless panties.

"Always wear pretty underwear, on account of, you just never know." - *Jill Conner Browne*

"Life is like underwear, should be changed twice a day." - *Ray Bradbury*

V

Versatility

TO BE VERSATILE IS defined in dictionary.com as being: "capable of or adapted for turning easily from one to another of various tasks, fields of endeavour, etc.: having or capable of many uses"

In etiquette and social graces, a versatile person is one can adapt their behaviour wherever they are to suit the occasion or circumstance.

Please note that being versatile is not the same thing as being pretentious.

Being versatile ensures success in relationships with people. In terms of social relationships, be prepared to accept opinions and cultures that are different from your own.

"Whatever it takes for me to win, I'm down for it. Versatility goes a long way. The person who is most versatile has more going for him than a guy who does just one thing." - *Barbara Morgan*

"Versatility increases your sphere of influence." - *Olu Adeaga*

Visiting

IF YOU ARE PLANNING on visiting someone, i.e. friends, family, acquaintances, etc., it is advisable to call ahead and not show up unannounced. People may be polite enough not to turn you away when you just land on their doorstep, however, think about how you feel when someone just shows up at your door without telling you they intended to visit.

It is also courteous (where possible) to take a gift for the person or family you are visiting; that will make them appreciate your visit even more.

Unless in an emergency, endeavour not to visit people before 9 am or after 9 pm.

Do not overstay your welcome; be discerning and know when to leave.

> **"Don't visit your neighbours too often; they may get tired of you and come to hate you."**
> - **Bible quote** (Proverbs 25:17, Good News Translation)

Volume

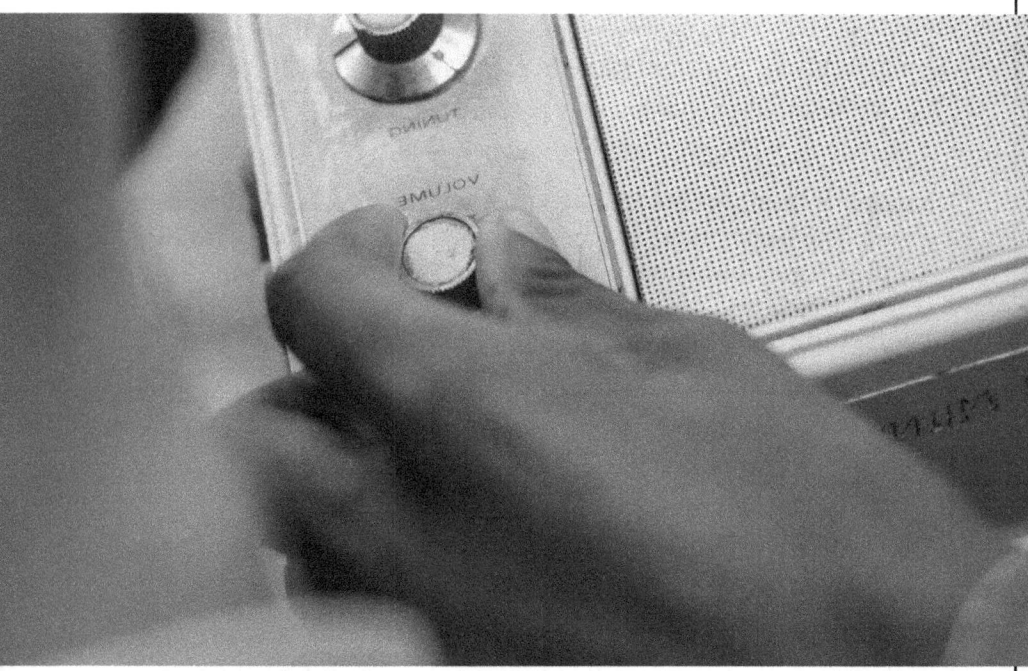

YOU HAVE PROBABLY HEARD the phrase "Keep the volume down" more times than you can count. Noise pollution is real and we happen to live in an environment where the noise levels are simply outrageous. Take care not to contribute to it.

Excessive noise levels can be annoying, and this has been known to affect our health, behaviour and relationships.

Keep the volume low when using the following:
- Air pods.
- Television.
- Mobile phone.
- Radio.
- Avoid using the horn on your vehicle, except if it is vital (i.e. to prevent an accident).
- When having a conversation or talking on your phone in public.
- Do not shout across a room/road/hallway etc, unless necessary.
- Kindly keep the volume down when having a conversation on public transportation. I recently suffered a 6-hour ordeal listening to a passenger having a conversation with her child and friend on a flight. By the end of the flight, I knew more about her than I cared to know. Interestingly, she was seated 6 rows behind me. I imagined how other passengers who were seated around her would have felt.
- Lastly, keep the volume of your laughter down when in public.

"The volume of your voice does not increase the validity of your argument." - *Steve Maraboli*

Wardrobe Maintenance

IF YOU SPEND MONEY on clothes, you owe it to yourself to look after them properly.

- Do not spray perfume on clothes.
- Hang clothes properly and do not drape them over the wardrobe doors. Make sure the clothes are not crowded in the wardrobe space.
- Fold clothes that need to be folded neatly.
- Make sure you read the 'care' instruction labels on your clothing. If the garment label states dry clean only, take it to a professional dry cleaner. If hand washing or using the machine, ensure that you wash at the right temperature, as per the manufacturer's instructions. Your wool clothing will shrink if

washed at hot temperatures. Make sure you separate clothes into colours and fabrics before washing.
- Ensure that zippers are fastened.
- Clean your shoes before storing them.
- Do not store dirty clothes with clean ones. Have a laundry basket for your dirty clothes.
- Organise your clothes so that the garments you wear often are at the front and you can easily access them.
- You can also organise your clothes by colours or items, e.g. all skirts together, etc.
- Jumpers and sweaters should be folded flat in a cool place.

> "Care for your clothes, like the good friends they are."
> - Joan Crawford

Wedding Etiquette

WEDDING ETIQUETTE COVERS SUCH a vast area, all of which cannot be covered here. I will, therefore, focus on a few areas that are traditional and modern.
- Make sure that invitation cards are sent out as early as possible.
- If you do not want children at the wedding, clearly state this on the invitation (somewhere at the bottom) and make sure it is worded properly and apologetically. Avoid stating, "No children allowed", as this can come across as too blunt and insensitive. It is better to say something along the lines of: "Please accept our apologies; however, we are unable to accommodate children at the reception".
- Also, make sure there is an RSVP with a name, number and date on the invitation.
- If you have received an invitation to a wedding, courtesy

demands that you respond before the date stated on the card. Even if you are close to the couple, do not assume that they know you will be attending. You must respond to allow them to plan for the date and to let the caterers know the number of people that will be attending.

- If you have been invited to a wedding church service, try not to be late. It is considered rude to walk in after the bride or even just as she is about to walk down the aisle.
- At the reception, if you have been allocated seats, do not move name places around. Remember that a lot of time and effort has probably gone into the arrangements.

(See the sections on 'Dress Etiquette' and 'Dining Etiquette')

"The real act of marriage takes place in the heart, not in the ballroom or church or synagogue. It's a choice you make - not just on your wedding day, but also over and over again - and that choice is reflected in the way you treat your husband or wife."
- Barbara de Angelis

X

Xenophobia

XENOPHOBIA IS A STRONG dislike or fear of people from other countries. It is defined in the Oxford and Webster dictionaries as: "Intense or irrational dislike or fear of people from other countries, or as an unreasonable fear or hatred of foreigners or strangers or of that which is foreign or strange."

As described, this fear is often unfounded. The rules of etiquette dictate that, even when we do not understand other people, we should at least be tolerant of them and show them respect and consideration.

To overcome this fear, we need to educate ourselves about other cultures and try to understand their beliefs and the reasons why they act or behave the way they do. It is often the case that when we make a conscious effort to understand others, we can get along well with them.

"I do not believe, from what I have been told about these people, that there is anything barbarous or savage about them, except that we all call barbarous anything that is contrary to our own habits."
- Michel de Montaigne

Xmas

THE FIRST THING TO note here is that the correct spelling is not 'Xmas'; the correct spelling is actually 'Christmas'. In this age of abbreviating everything, certain words and terms lose their meaning when abbreviated. Christians celebrate Christmas because it signifies the birth of Jesus Christ; hence the essence of Christmas is Christ.

Christmas can be a very stressful period if you do not prepare months in advance; from deciding on what presents to buy, to whom you should invite over for Christmas dinner, or which invitations you can decline and which one you should accept. For the employed, there is also the office Christmas party to get through; and the list goes on.

Planning is the key to surviving the Christmas period.

- Do not overspend on Christmas presents; if you cannot afford it, do not buy it. Avoid maxing out your credit card or getting an overdraft or borrowing, just so you can please everyone.
- If possible, buy your Christmas presents months earlier during the sale period.
- Give yourself plenty of time to think about what to buy for each person.
- If your finances are a little tight, look for creative ways to make presents. Remember, it is the thought that counts.
- Unfortunately, we cannot choose who we are related to, so you may not have much of a choice in whom to invite over for Christmas.
- If family members always come over to yours for Christmas, come up with a good reason to have it at another family member's home next Christmas. Again, give plenty of notice, so that the family can prepare.
- It is not a good idea to avoid office Christmas parties. Declining an invitation for the office Christmas party can come across as though you do not want to socialise with your colleagues and it may appear as though you are not invested in the company you work for.

"My idea of Christmas, whether old-fashioned or modern, is very simple: loving others. Come to think of it, why do we have to wait for Christmas to do that?" - *Bob Hope*

Y

Yawning

IT IS HUMAN NATURE to yawn sometimes. We yawn as a result of lack of sleep, tiredness or boredom. Most times, it is involuntary and often catches us unawares.

If you feel a yawn coming, especially when you are in a public place, try to yawn with your mouth closed. If that is not possible, then put your hand over your mouth.

Yawning when you are with other people or in a business meeting can be perceived as a sign of boredom or lack of interest.

"Yawning is like our bodies way of saying 15% battery left."
– Anonymous

"Never yawn in front of a lady." *– Frank Sinatra*

Yes

'YES' IS MEANT TO be a positive response or assent, but if not accompanied by the appropriate expression, it loses its meaning and effectiveness. For example, when responding to a question, the etiquette of saying 'yes' requires simply adding the word 'please'. Saying 'Yes please' is pleasing, polite and sends a positive message of affirmation to people.

In a restaurant, a waiter will ask if you would like a drink. Whilst the waiter is paid to serve you and is doing their duty, responding with 'Yes please' is a sign of regard for the waiter, regardless of their status or duty. The right response invariably provokes even better service, as they feel respected and appreciated.

"My mother used to tell me, "No matter what they ask you, always say yes. You can learn later." - *Natalie Wood*

Z

Zeal

TO HAVE ZEAL IS defined as having: "Fervor for a person, cause, or object; eager desire or endeavour; enthusiastic diligence; ardour." – *dictionary.com*

Do you not just love being around people who are full of zeal? They are a joy and a delight to be around. Life is full of enough challenges without someone adding to the misery of others with their apathy.

As much as is within your power, try to be a zealous person even about the simple things in life. People will be drawn to you like a magnet.

"Experience shows that success is due less to ability than to zeal."
- Charles Buxton

"The most important thing women have to do is to stir up the zeal of women themselves." - John Stuart Mill

Zebra Crossings

IN 1949, ZEBRA CROSSINGS were first introduced in the UK as a means whereby pedestrians could safely cross the road. The Highway Code rules 191 to 195 deal with the guidelines regarding zebra crossings. The bottom line is that the pedestrian has the right of way at a zebra crossing. A motorist approaching the crossing has to slow down and should not move forward until the pedestrian has crossed over to the other side of the road.

Although it is not written in the Code, as a sign of courtesy, pedestrians should either wave or nod to the motorist who has stopped at the zebra crossing for them to get across the road.

Also, note that, as a cyclist, you are meant to dismount when you want to cross a zebra crossing.

> **"Pedestrians never seem to realize that they are a threat to the safety of cars."** - *Thomas Sowell*

Zips

THE QUESTION TO ASK is this; if your zipper was down, would you like to be told? A courteous person who notices that a man or woman's zipper is down should discretely point it out to the person; this will save them from further embarrassment. Avoid telling them in front of other people or shouting it out loud. If you can, pull the person to the side and tell them. Do not smile or laugh when you tell them because they will already be embarrassed.

"Nobody notices it when your zipper is up, but everyone notices when it's down." - *Cynthia Lewis*

Conclusion

When all is said and done, the most important thing to remember regarding etiquette is that it is about having consideration for others; it is about being aware of your surroundings; noticing the little things that will make a difference in the life of another person.

Lastly, it is about extending yourself by going the extra mile.

If we all commit to doing this, perhaps the world would be a slightly better place to live.

Thank you for reading.

About the Author

Olu Adeaga holds two Bachelor's degrees in History and Law; and a Master's degree in Christian Mentoring. After completing her Law degree, she commenced her early career in the Finance sector, but later pursued her dream of establishing JSapphirah, a unique establishment designing and manufacturing ladies' shirts.

Olu is passionate about encouraging, developing and empowering women. She was instrumental in establishing a formal mentoring programme for women called Esthers' Mentoring Scheme (EMS) and is also the founder of the Christian Mentoring Association.

From a very young age, Olu has been passionate about the 'proper way to behave' in social interactions. She believes the world would be a much better place if we all learned and applied social skills and graces, as well as comported ourselves appropriately and practised being considerate of others.

She has since become renowned as a practitioner and teacher of Etiquette, and has conducted training on Etiquette for numerous organisations and ministries. She also believes in the complete woman; one who is spiritually developed, astute and well turned out, and her message is that a woman should maximise each season of her life.

Olu enjoys travelling and reading. She is married with 2 children.

www.ingramcontent.com/pod-product-compliance
Lightning Source LLC
Chambersburg PA
CBHW022110090426
42743CB00008B/799